AF865741

We Are Called to Rise

The Power of Refugee Women

We Are Called to Rise

JINA KRAUSE-VILMAR

MOMENT OF LIFT BOOKS
FLATIRON BOOKS
NEW YORK

This is a work of nonfiction. However, the author has used pseudonyms for the first names of most of the women and men mentioned by name in the book.

WE ARE CALLED TO RISE. Copyright © 2026 by Jina Krause-Vilmar. All rights reserved. Printed in the United States of America. For information, address Flatiron Books, 120 Broadway, New York, NY 10271. EU Representative: Macmillan Publishers Ireland Ltd., 1st Floor, The Liffey Trust Centre, 117–126 Sheriff Street Upper, Dublin 1, D01 YC43.

www.flatironbooks.com

Designed by Leah Carlson-Stanisic

Illustration by TaniKoArt / Shutterstock

The Library of Congress Cataloging-in-Publication Data is available upon request.

ISBN 978-1-250-82802-6 (hardcover)
ISBN 978-1-250-82804-0 (ebook)

The publisher of this book does not authorize the use or reproduction of any part of this book in any manner for the purpose of training artificial intelligence technologies or systems. The publisher of this book expressly reserves this book from the Text and Data Mining exception in accordance with Article 4(3) of the European Union Digital Single Market Directive 2019/790.

Our books may be purchased in bulk for specialty retail/wholesale, literacy, corporate/premium, educational, and subscription box use. Please contact MacmillanSpecialMarkets@macmillan.com.

First Edition: 2026

10 9 8 7 6 5 4 3 2 1

To my mother, husband,
and children

Contents

Part 3
COLLECTIVE ACTION

Introduction

We live in a time when seeking safety is treated as a crime, when the movement of displaced people is weaponized for political gain, and the humanity of refugees is stripped away. Those fleeing wars, persecution, and climate catastrophe are cast as threats rather than survivors of unimaginable hardship. Across the world—from Germany to India to Brazil—right-wing movements are gaining power by scapegoating the most vulnerable. On January 27, 2025, the United States suspended refugee admissions, defunded aid to refugee camps, and on February 4 halted funding to the United Nations High Commissioner for Refugees (UNHCR), which, in 2024, received more than 40 percent of its nearly $5 billion budget from the United States. These decisions have real consequences for real lives. But who are these people? Who fills the categories that policies erase?

As humans, we possess a singular gift: the ability to create and believe in shared stories, those intersubjective myths that exist only because we agree they do. These collective imaginations make possible the systems that govern our world: the nation-state, economies, the rule of law, and even the very notion of human rights. But when certain people's stories are missing, especially women's, the foundations of our shared reality begin to fracture. Without women's stories, we lose sight of how communities are sustained, how economies function, how societies endure. Nowhere is this erasure more striking than in the narratives we tell about refugee women.

Their stories are too often cast in the narrow light of victimhood: helpless, dependent, waiting to be saved. Yet, refugee women are master strategists, navigating complex systems with intention, skill, and extraordinary resilience. They are not merely surviving crisis; they are shaping the possibilities that follow it. To reclaim their stories is to expand our understanding of what is possible, and to reimagine the systems that define our shared humanity.

This narrative problem leads to a resource problem. Funding follows what a society values, and society values only what it sees and understands. Refugee women remain largely invisible. That invisibility is no longer acceptable, not simply because it is unjust, but because when the most vulnerable rise, we all rise.

My understanding of invisibility, of being overlooked, underestimated, and pushed to the margins, began long before my work with refugees. I grew up in poverty, raised by a single mother, a newly arrived Indian immigrant in a conservative Baptist community in Texas. My mom faced every possible obstacle: the weight of being a woman, an outsider, and a single parent. She worked three low-wage jobs, navigating a world that routinely dismissed her value.

As a child, I wondered why women like my mother had to prove themselves endlessly. Why was her labor treated as less valuable? My father refused to pay for child support, and the courts looked away. When she tried to restart her teaching career, her master's degree from India was dismissed.

Later, parents at the high school where she taught complained that a "foreigner" couldn't teach English literature. Again and again, the message was the same: Know your place and be grateful for it.

As I got older, I came to understand what I could not name at the time: the ways my mother's ethnicity, gender, class, and immigration status converged to produce a distinct experience of exclusion. These intersecting identities shaped the opportunities available to her, the judgments cast upon her, and the ways she was seen, or not seen, by those around her.

Meanwhile, those who did not live at similar intersections, my friends' parents, my teachers, and later my coworkers, struggled to recognize discrimination unless it arrived with irrefutable data. When I shared that my mother had once been questioned by police while waiting in a friend's driveway, a coworker insisted it must have been a misunderstanding. When I was repeatedly singled out for security checks at the Berlin airport, a friend suggested it was because I was "pretty." The absence of proof does not mean the absence of truth. Oppression is not always neatly measured. Sometimes we know because we feel it. Because we carry it. Because we live it.

Where there is oppression, there is also power, unshared, concentrated, often invisible. I grew up trying to understand it. My mother, who grew up in a British Catholic school in India, filled our home with stories and authors she loved, Dickens, Shakespeare, Elizabeth Gaskell, Thomas Hardy, Wilkie Collins, and P. G. Wodehouse, that shaped my early understanding of class, struggle, and human nature. But books weren't the only thing that shaped me.

Because my mother worked three jobs, I spent much of my childhood with my grandfather, a military man, a wing commander who had fought in World War II and served in the Indian Air Force in conflicts with Pakistan and China. He and I had a ritual: We'd watch *Star Trek: The Next Generation* together every night, exploring the politics of culture. He taught me to have relentless curiosity, quizzing my sisters and me from the *Encyclopedia Britannica* about history and geopolitics. Together, these influences taught me that power is not only written about in books—it moves through systems, institutions, and the stories we accept as truth.

Still, it would take more than a decade of working alongside refugee women, designing and implementing economic programs across continents, partnering with the U.S. Department of State, USAID, the United Nations, and leading humanitarian organizations, for me to truly see how power operates. How it excludes. How it reshapes destinies. And how, with intention, it can be reimagined.

Power is embedded in the very fabric of displacement. I have sat in refugee camps where families waited years, sometimes decades, for a future they were not sure would come, determined entirely by decisions made far away. I have met asylum seekers whose skills and experiences could transform industries, if only systems allowed them the chance. And I have witnessed communities revitalize when refugees are permitted to contribute and reclaim their power.

Yet today, doors are closing. Aid is evaporating. Employers are retreating. And still people flee, because they must.

This book is about the economic power of refugee women: the power policymakers overlook, governments fail to harness, and stereotypes erase. It is about the opportunities lost when we reduce refugee women to victims instead of recognizing them as economic drivers and leaders. Over the past twenty years, I have listened to women who are building futures in the spaces where systems fail them. Their stories, paired with the research, policy insights, and lived experiences, offer a framework for reimagining how societies can shift.

This book is meant to give readers the tools to rethink and reshape the systems and culture we collectively create. It moves between big ideas and practical solutions—from the individual power each of us holds to the collective power we can build—to reshape the narratives that shape our world.

Because here is the truth: When the most vulnerable rise, we all rise.

The question facing us now is simple—and urgent: Will we continue to turn our backs, or will we open the door?

PART 1

The New Frontier

1

Upended Gender Norms

The taxi sliced through the sleeping streets of Nairobi, its headlights carving a narrow path through the dark. It was 2016, and I was on my way to Thigiri, an upscale neighborhood where mansions sat on acres of manicured lawns and gardens bordered by bougainvillea hedges. When we stopped, the driver drummed his fingers on the steering wheel, waiting for the guards behind the iron gate to notice us. Two men emerged, their faded brown uniforms dissolving into the shadows. One glanced at the driver, asking who I was. I leaned forward, met the guard's gaze, and gave my own name.

The guard lazily scanned his clipboard. "You're not on the list."

A list? I frowned. "Is this where Matteo and Beatrice live? They have two small children—Rachael and Dani?"

"Yes," came the disinterested reply.

Relief flickered. At least I was in the right place.

"You can let me in," I said. "I'm their friend from the United States, staying with them."

He repeated, flatly, "You're not on the list."

I started to hate this list.

"Could you knock on the door and ask them?" I said, leaning forward, my eyes on the house just beyond the gate, fifteen paces away, lights off, perfectly still. The guards murmured to each other in Kiswahili. One finally nodded, trudged to the door, and rapped once. Silence. He waited for a beat, then turned back. Nothing.

The man with the clipboard looked at me, his face impassive, tone indifferent. "They are asleep."

The situation was starting to tilt. It hadn't occurred to me that my friends might have a full security detail or that it could stand so firmly between me and them. Insistent panic crept in. I had no plan B. Just the gate, the dark, and the realization that I was utterly alone in a country that wasn't mine.

"Can you call their cell phone?" I called out, my voice tightening.

The taxi driver turned in his seat, his eyes decisive. "I'll have to take you to a hotel," he said. "It's not safe to leave you here."

His tone was firm, almost fatherly. But as the car idled before the iron gate, I felt the truth settle: I wasn't getting in.

After the long flight from New York, exhaustion folded over me. Still, I knew how this story could go—the taxi driver delivers you to a seedy hotel where he gets a small kickback from the manager. I was a woman traveling alone. I knew the calculus of risk. Best case: a few crude remarks, a lingering gaze that stripped away any pretense of safety. Worst case: something far darker waiting behind a locked hotel door. Nope, no way. I declined before he could finish his sentence. I didn't know where I was, and if my phone died, no one else would either. I just needed to get into that damn house.

Okay, time to roll up my sleeves. All that stood between me and a safe night's sleep were these two guards. I eyed the towering wall surrounding the property. Maybe I could scale it? Just me, I'd need to leave the suitcase behind. Or I could scream my friends' names, I wasn't above acts of desperation. No, best start with pleading and see if that gets me anywhere first.

So, I started talking. Fast. I told them how I'd met Beatrice and Matteo back in Brooklyn. Beatrice and I were new moms together, our babies born days apart, bonded by sleep deprivation. I rambled about playdates in shoebox apartments and daycare pickups that ended when they moved to Nairobi for Matteo's United Nations post.

Five minutes into my entreaty, the side door creaked open. Matteo appeared in pajamas, fumbling with his glasses, hair tousled, face slack with sleep. Hallelujah, relief hit like a wave as the gate groaned open.

Crisis averted.

I stepped out of the car, moved past the guards and the outer gate, and passed through the side door, itself protected by its own smaller iron lattice gate. I breathed out, the tension in my shoulders released. The house was suspended between time and memory with a ceiling that soared upward, their edges softened by the amber glow of dim lights overhead. Polished wooden floors gleamed like honey beneath my feet, reflecting the slow, soft hum of the ceiling fans. French doors lined a far wall, opening onto a wraparound veranda where the night's breath carried the faint perfume of jasmine flowers. Beyond, a garden melded into shadow, its foliage swaying gently.

As I sank into that relief, a subtle tension began to creep up my spine. The house's colonial bones carried an undeniable sense of vigilance; a quiet watchfulness layered beneath the beauty.

We climbed the staircase, each step creaking softly underfoot, until we reached the sleeping quarters. At the top, another iron gate awaited, its cold metallic clang reverberating in the still night as Matteo locked it behind us. He led me to the guest room, which had tall windows with wrought-iron bars twisted into intricate patterns. The room felt both welcoming and wary, a strange blend of hospitality and caution.

Beside the door, set into the wall, a small red button caught my eye. A call bell? No way, room service?!

"What's this for?" I asked, hopeful.

"It's a panic button," Matteo replied, his tone calm. "Every room has one."

Every room? I swallowed hard, the unease in my chest growing. "Matteo," I whispered, "what exactly is going to happen to us?"

He shrugged, nonchalantly. "Theft is common in Nairobi," as if that explained everything.

The next morning, after a safe night's sleep, I set out to take in the city. I arrived in Nairobi, notebook in hand, leading a global research project exploring which assets help refugees survive and, hopefully, thrive. I came equipped with all the right tools: surveys like the Household Economy Analysis, packed with smart questions about food, income, and assets. On paper, it looked solid. But pretty quickly, I realized that real understanding doesn't come from ticking boxes about how many meals someone eats, what kind of food they can afford, or putting price tags on their few household items. It comes from listening as people describe their day-to-day, how their routines shift, and why getting by is so hard. To do that, you have to let go of assumptions.

It's easy to interpret someone else's choices through the framework of your own experience. But our experiences aren't neutral, they're shaped by how other people see us and respond to us.

When you move through the world with various kinds of privilege, many social interactions feel seamless. You may not even register them as interactions at all. If you've never struggled to get a taxi to stop, it can seem like transportation is simply a matter of raising your hand. But if you're someone who is regularly profiled, assumed to be poor, or discriminated against, that same moment carries a different weight. A driver passing you by is part of a pattern. The experience sits differently because the social meaning around it is different.

The key point is reflection. When you're not exposed to certain barriers, they can be invisible. And when you do encounter friction, you may interpret it as an isolated inconvenience rather than part of a broader dynamic. Someone else, living in a different social reality, may reasonably interpret that same friction as discrimination because that interpretation is consistent with their repeated experience.

Understanding this requires recognizing that your vantage point is partial. It means asking open, genuinely curious questions and listening for context and the "why"—the trade-offs people are making, the risks they're managing, the small adjustments they've learned to survive within systems that don't treat everyone equally.

This kind of understanding develops slowly. It's not about collecting facts; it's about recognizing that two people can encounter the same social norm and experience it very differently because the world responds to them differently. When you grasp that, conversations shift from debating whether something "should" feel discriminatory to understanding why, for someone else, it does.

The project was in partnership with UNHCR, the UN agency that makes sure refugees have somewhere safe to go, and can access food, water, shelter, and medical care. They also work to protect displaced people's rights, so they're not mistreated or sent back into danger. Beyond that, they help people figure out the long game: returning home when it's safe, resettling in a third country, or building a new life where they are.

My research focused on safe livelihoods for urban refugees. Safety matters because arriving in a new city is about surviving in an unfamiliar, often unwelcoming place. Many people, especially women, juggle the reality of being uprooted while trying to feed and protect their families with few legal options to earn a living. That gap leaves them exposed to all kinds of dangers, like gender-based violence.

In fact, around one in three women and girls face gender-based violence.[1] Exploitative employers, predatory clients, even police can inflict physical and sexual harm, meanwhile desperation pushes some women toward dangerous coping strategies—like exchanging sex for food or shelter.

In 1963, Kenya gained independence from British colonial rule, ending nearly seventy years of foreign occupation. Today, it is sub-Saharan Africa's fourth-largest economy. Nairobi, the "Silicon Savannah," operates as a modern economic hub driven by an AI boom, mobile technology, digital banking, and innovative payment systems. But even with all that progress, colonialism hangs in the background. The old colonial system of land grabs, forced labor, and concentrated power among a select few has left deep inequalities that haven't disappeared. When I was there, most Kenyans were trapped in low-paying, unstable jobs, in farming or the informal economy, without real access to education or tech opportunities. So, while Kenya's tech and fintech scene was booming, that progress wasn't lifting everyone.

The divide was impossible to miss. On one side of Nairobi sprawled overcrowded shantytowns, where necessities like sanitation, clean water, and electricity were scarce. Between 60 and 70 percent of Nairobi residents lived in these slums.[2] On the other, gleaming gated communities flaunted modern infrastructure, manicured lawns, and high-end shopping malls. Two realities resting in uneasy proximity.

Surrounded by countries like Somalia, South Sudan, and Ethiopia, all of which have faced war and unrest, Kenya was a natural destination for those fleeing conflict, persecution, and instability across East Africa.

And because 78 percent of the world's refugees live in cities rather than camps,[3] Nairobi was a prime destination. Women and girls arrive with few resources, separated from family members, in countries that largely do not want them. They typically settle alongside the urban poor struggling to survive, in environments where resources are scarce and competition runs high. With more than half the world's refugees (55 percent) legally restricted from securing work, despite it being an internationally recognized right,[4] exploitation and discrimination are rampant.

Sitting tensely in the back of that taxi, on the wrong side of the gate, I didn't have a plan B, but I did have a safety net: a credit card, a cell phone, a U.S. passport, and an embassy to lean on. The urban refugees I had come to learn from had none of that. Every question I asked, every note I took, was framed by that stark contrast, the distance between my security and the constant precarity of the lives I intended to understand and support.

I met Aamina through a local refugee-serving organization. She welcomed me into her one-room flat, a small space she shared with her two children and a young Congolese woman named Grace. Despite the cramped quarters, dirt floor, and leaky tin roof, the home was tidy and meticulously kept. The only furniture consisted of two step stools, a pair of bunk beds pressed against the teal-gray walls, and a *mitad*, a large, round, flat cookstove resembling a circular griddle.

Aamina sat on a small wooden stool; its legs strained under her weight. Her broad shoulders were rigid, carrying the quiet strength of someone who had endured more than most. She was in her mid-forties, and streaks of gray now threaded through her wiry hair. Her gaze held a steady, unwavering calm. When she spoke, it was measured—direct, without bitterness.

In 2007, she had landed in Eastleigh, a sprawling Nairobi slum, after fleeing Ethiopia under the cover of night. Her husband had been killed by Ethiopian security forces for his ties to an opposition party daring to challenge Meles Zenawi's ruling Ethiopian People's Revolutionary Democratic Front coalition. By 2010, the coalition had secured 99 percent of Ethiopia's 3.4 million local and national elected seats, making dissent a dangerous game.[5] Fear had driven her into the darkness. Aamina gathered her ailing mother and two young sons, leaving behind everything.

The journey to Kenya was grueling, 750 kilometers on

foot, roughly the distance from New York City to Cleveland, Ohio. Most people fleeing conflict ended up in refugee camps, but Aamina had hesitated to settle there. She'd heard the stories about Kakuma, a remote refugee camp in Kenya's northwest where tents stretched endlessly across the sunbaked desert. Built as a temporary refuge in 1992, it had grown to house over 120,000 people[6]—almost double its intended capacity. Generations had been born there, trapped in limbo behind fences built to keep people in, dependent on food rations and permission to move.

Aamina knew that life in the camp offered little chance to work. She worried her mother wouldn't get the medical care she needed, and once inside, they might never get back out.

"It's not a place you choose," a fellow refugee woman told her. "It's where you end up when you have no other options." Refugee camps are set up as temporary solutions to urgent crises, and they're built that way, fast, with lightweight materials like tents, tarps, and sheet metal structures. Managed by a mix of national government, UNHCR, and humanitarian organizations, they provide the bare essentials—food, water, healthcare, education—and are often organized into zones or blocks to streamline services and control population flow.

Freedom of movement is heavily restricted. You can't just walk out to visit a nearby village or look for work in a neighboring town. Leaving the camp often requires a government-issued permit, and many camp inhabitants don't get one. Inside, refugees form their own governance structures. Community-based committees (organized by ethnicity, nationality, or neighborhood) help mediate disputes, coordinate with aid agencies, and represent resident concerns. Women's groups and youth councils are often set up, too, advocating for their needs, as community-based committees are often led by elder men. But ultimate control remains external, with international agencies and host governments setting the rules, deciding resource allocation, and dictating movement.

These systems gave shape to daily life but couldn't soften the harder question each person faced: Could I build a life here, or would I be trapped by it? For Aamina, that question had loomed large.

On her journey through Kenya, Aamina met a woman who had lived in one of the camps. Aamina recounted how the refugee woman she had met tried to make a life in a similar camp, Dadaab. She had grown vegetables in her little kitchen garden and sold them at a makeshift stall on her designated plot of land. Slowly, other women began asking if they could bring their own produce, and she welcomed them, creating a small, shared marketplace. To make it work, they would need to expand the stall on her plot. They pooled their limited funds and approached the refugee leadership, asking if they could enlarge the space. The refugee leadership wouldn't allow it, even if it was within her own plot. The women spoke with the camp authorities and appealed their case. Eventually, they granted them permission. Encouraged, they spent what money they had saved on timber and iron sheets. But trouble came before the first nail was hammered.

Men from nearby stalls showed up at the woman's tent. "You can't do this," they warned. "Try and we will take steps against you." The next day, they did exactly that. As she stood in front of her stall, trying to protect her goods, they attacked. Fire swallowed everything, her stall, her tent, all of it, leaving only ash and rubble.

For Aamina, it was a stark lesson: Life in camp depended on the mercy of others, on aid distributions, on permission from camp authorities, and on the unpredictable whims of those in charge. Nairobi, though chaotic and unforgiving, held a different promise. In the city's crowded streets, Aamina could disappear. She could work, build, survive. It wasn't perfect, but at least, here, it was her choice.

She settled in Eastleigh, where the streets were choked with rubbish and dust. Aamina stood out: Her *kemis*, the traditional ankle-length Ethiopian dress, made her origin known before she ever spoke. It was one of the few pieces of clothing she had brought with her, a fragile link to the home she had lost. It was worn down but well maintained, its fabric softened by years of wear, its seams repeatedly stitched and reinforced with care.

She soon learned one of the most painful truths of displacement: Humanitarian aid is fleeting and fickle. Aid decreases over time. Donors shift their focus to the next crisis, the next catastrophe. Funding that once felt like a lifeline slowly dries up, even as the needs remain.

You see it everywhere. Take the start of the 2011 Syrian Civil War. At that time, humanitarian aid covered 68 percent of urgent needs for Syrians, both inside the country and in neighboring nations.[7] A decade later, that support had been cut in half,[8] leaving eight in ten Syrians in extreme poverty, unable to afford food.

Similarly, when war broke out in Ukraine in 2022, European nations redirected up to 40 percent of their aid away from Africa to support Ukrainian refugees.[9] In 2025, as conflicts and displacement surged worldwide, the U.S. government, UNHCR's largest donor, providing 40 percent of its budget, announced massive funding cuts, resulting in major reductions in refugee services.

When Aamina and her family first arrived in Eastleigh, help came in the form of aid from a local organization, the same UNHCR-funded group that had introduced us. While it was enough to scrape by, covering rent, two meals per day, and a few incidentals like soap, it was never truly enough to rebuild. Within the first year, the same month her mother died, the support stopped altogether.

I've seen this time and again; refugees who rely solely on nonprofit aid or a single income stream often fall into extreme poverty. When that support vanishes, they can't pay rent, they get evicted, they crowd into tiny rooms with other families, or worse, they end up on the street, surviving on one meal a day if they're lucky. Thriving depends on diversifying, on earning from multiple sources, because the moment one income stream is in jeopardy, everything unravels. When aid stops and fails to connect people to work or the skills to find it, we are simply offering a temporary lifeline with an expiration date, a fragile bridge stretched to an uncertain future, hoping people find their footing before it gives way.

Relying on a single source of support had left Aamina vulnerable. She had no plan B. So, she made one. After her mother's death, Aamina began selling secondhand shoes and clothing on the streets, her boys by her side. She washed dishes and did laundry for neighbors. On most days, they ate one meal of thin flatbread and lentils.

It didn't help that refugees weren't allowed to work outside designated camps. When she applied for asylum in Nairobi, she was granted the right to stay in the city while her case was processed, but not the right to work. It was a policy designed to deter refugees. A silent message: *Don't come here. And if you must come, don't stay*. One problem with that is that a refugee is a refugee on average for twenty years. How does someone survive that long without a livelihood? Aamina was caught between two impossible choices: return home and face prison as a political dissident or stay and risk starving. She chose to take her chances in the city's informal economy, blending into its restless pulse. It's a world made up of all the ways people earn outside official systems, street vending, domestic work, or small side hustles, without contracts, taxes, or legal protections. For many women refugees, it's not a choice so much as the only option.

And strikingly, it's the only option for the majority of the world's women. Fifty-eight percent of working women globally work in the informal economy: That's 95 percent of working women in South Asia, 89 percent in sub-Saharan Africa, and 59 percent in Latin America.[10]

So many women are stuck in informal work.

From the moment they are born, girls in societies all around the world are often seen as future mothers first, everything else second. The logic follows: If their destiny is simply to raise children, why bother educating them? Why prepare them for skilled work? This mindset sustains a self-perpetuating cycle—one that keeps women undereducated; confines them to low-wage, informal labor; and reinforces the false belief that they neither belong in formal employment nor deserve financial independence. For refugee women, these barriers harden into near immovable walls. Many are denied the legal right to work, and when opportunities do exist, their marginalized status funnels them into the most exploitative and poorly paid roles. There, they face higher rates of sexual harassment and are far more likely to have their wages withheld or stolen by their employer.

Aamina no longer received aid and relied on the informal economy. She had learned that households with only one source of income were vulnerable: Children were often pulled from school to help earn money, and in times of desperation families turned to churches or mosques for shelter and food. Those with multiple income streams through petty trading, home-based production, or informal labor were better able to weather financial shocks. They still lived with uncertainty, but they had options. Aamina's goal was to be in that latter category.

Morning settled quietly in Aamina's small home. The warm, slightly sour aroma of injera, a spongy Ethiopian flatbread, perfumed the room, mingling uneasily with the foul air of raw sewage creeping in from the alley outside. Dawn had barely broken, and the children still slept. Aamina sat on a stool, encircled by large plastic bowls covered with thin, frayed kitchen towels. Grace stood nearby, kneading dough with gentle, practiced efficiency. I rested on the second stool, my back against the wall, and watched the day slowly gather itself.

Grace had curious eyes, a lean frame, a quiet smile. She wore the traditional Congolese fabric, kitenge, draped like a sarong around her chest and waist. Today, it was a vibrant green material with bold geometric patterns, a striking contrast to the faded walls.

Aamina broke the hazy silence: "The early hours are best for cooking." Her hands never paused. "Otherwise, the tin roof bakes us in this heat."

"I deliver the injera to local shops and hotels nearby. Always nearby. It's not much money, but it's enough." Her eyes remained fixed on her task, as she spoke. "Of course, the money I get changes. Rainy season is no good. Elections are no good. Sometimes I struggle to pay rent or school fees. I pay the girl [Grace] when I can."

Aamina still washed dishes and laundry, while Grace sold used shoes and clothing on the street. Inside their home, there was a momentary ease. Outside, both women were on edge, bodies tense, eyes sharp, watching the men who drifted too close. The constant threat of harassment kept them from moving freely, limiting where they could go and ultimately how many customers they could reach.

And then there were the police. In 2010, some officers turned harassment into a profitable business by regularly extorting bribes from refugees. It didn't matter if you were registered with the government. Releasing a detained husband or son could cost up to 300,000 Kenyan shillings, about 2,300 U.S. dollars, a sum that would take most families three years to save. Because police were less likely to arrest women and children for cultural reasons, families often sent them out to sell goods, believing it was the safer option. But safety was relative. Instead of arrest, women faced other dangers, harassment, demands for sex, and customers who knew they could get away without paying.

Aamina explained the system of extortion to me the way one might explain the weather. "When you cannot pay the bribe, they take whatever you have. The injera I just made. The groceries I just bought. Fridays are the worst. The police need extra cash for their weekend."

When I was sixteen, my first job was as a cashier at a Walgreens in the suburbs of Houston. It wasn't glamorous, mostly scanning cough medicine and stocking toilet paper, but it gave me something I'd never had before: my own paycheck. Growing up, I had always felt guilty asking my mom for money. I knew how hard she worked, stretching every dollar to cover rent, groceries, and school supplies. So, I usually didn't ask for anything. I remember feeling a quiet thrill every time I clocked in at work. For weeks, I saved up with one goal in mind, to buy a deep red, faux-leather hooded motorcycle jacket. It was bold and nothing I needed, but that was the point. That jacket was more than a purchase. It represented the first time I felt the freedom to want something just because. I didn't have to justify it. I didn't have to worry if it made someone else's life harder. I just wanted it. And I could choose it.

Back then, I thought earning your own money meant freedom. But working with refugee women taught me something different: Having an income doesn't always mean having the power to choose.

As in Kenya, most Syrian refugees in Jordan had no legal right to work. They were only permitted home-based businesses, like soapmaking, tailoring, and small-scale food production, but these ventures rarely earned enough to sustain an entire family. In 2014, two in three Syrian[11] refugees lived below the poverty line, compared to just 15 percent of Jordanians.[12] Only 2 percent of Syrian households could afford basic food without resorting to harmful coping strategies like child labor, early marriage, or prostitution.[13] It's the result of systems that refuse to open safer alternatives.

In Irbid, industrial factories pressed up against the fertile farmland of the Jordan Valley. Syria lay just beyond the horizon, twelve miles away. It was here that I met Yassi. The city teemed with 1.9 million people, its Roman ruins and the Jordan University of Science and Technology hinting at continuity and progress. But, for families like Yassi's it was a place of limbo, a place shaped less by possibility than by calculations of survival.

Yassi was ten, but carried herself with the poise of someone much older. She had a small, delicately featured face and a careful way about her, the kind of child who would break a cookie in half to save some for later. She lived with her family on the fifth floor of a crumbling apartment building, in rooms accessible only by stairs. The hallway walls, stripped of paint, revealed the bare concrete beneath. Laundry fluttered on makeshift lines hung out of windows. In the narrow corridors, I heard the muffled hum of voices, women exchanging midday gossip.

Yassi's mother had received a small grant from my organization to start a home-based catering business. The living space was nearly bare, save for two thin mattresses on the floor, where I took a seat and offered a box of Turkish delights and a bag of fresh fruit. The fruit vanished into the kitchen, where Yassi's two older sisters, fourteen and fifteen, remained out of sight. The mother joined me on the mattress, savoring the Turkish delights.

The family had arrived in Jordan three years earlier, after the Syrian war began. In a different world, Yassi would have been in school. Instead, she worked twelve-hour shifts in a bakery—7 a.m. to 7 p.m., seven days a week, for just five dinars a day, the equivalent of seven U.S. dollars. It was half of Jordan's minimum wage and barely enough to feed one person, but for Yassi's family, it stretched to cover everyone.

Despite the grueling hours, they all agreed that any job was better than no job. Whenever the police came to inspect the bakery, Yassi pretended to be a customer to avoid arrest.

"I work twelve hours a day every single day, and it's hard work," she told me. "You don't get a day off unless you ask for one, and then they don't pay you. Sometimes they ask me to stay later. During Ramadan, I didn't get home until one in the morning."

She spoke pragmatically. "I couldn't find another job that paid more. Of course, they take advantage of us because we are refugees. They don't treat Jordanians this way; they put them in a better position." She absentmindedly twirled a loose thread from her shirt. "We lived a better life in Syria," she mused and then said matter-of-factly, "but things changed. So, we have to work."

Before the war, her father owned two factories, but his pro-democratic stance led to torture by the Syrian government, leaving him paralyzed from the waist down. Yassi's mother, eager to have her share of the conversation, interjected, "We left Syria, and within hours, our house was demolished, my uncle killed, and our entire life left behind." She leaned back against the wall, exhaling slowly. "We can stand being hungry," she said. "But we cannot live without a roof over our heads." With the head of household unable to work, every family member had to make difficult choices.

Between bites of Turkish delight, Yassi's mother nonchalantly described how she had arranged marriages for her two eldest daughters to older Jordanian men. In Syria, while early marriage existed before the war, it was never widespread. Only 12 percent of Syrian girls married before turning eighteen—but during the war, that number more than doubled to nearly one in four marriages.[14] Economic desperation left few open paths, and it extracted a devastating cost. These girls' safety, their future, was the price of survival.

"We received some dowry, which helped pay the rent," she explained, popping another Turkish delight into her mouth. She didn't say it outright, but the reality was clear—fewer mouths to feed. Even with the dowry money, the family was still drowning in debt. They owed their landlord a staggering one thousand dollars in overdue rent, an amount that felt like an impossible weight to lift.

In some communities, marriage carries deep social meaning. It's tied to family honor, social acceptance, and stability. For many families facing conflict, poverty, or displacement, marrying off a daughter early can feel like a form of protection, a way to secure her safety in an unpredictable world.

For a long time, I saw early marriage only through one lens. My mother's arranged marriage had been difficult, and I grew up believing that such arrangements were proof of how little value society placed on women and girls. It felt like girls were treated as something to be traded or sold off like cattle. Over time, I learned that it can be more complicated than that. The reasons behind early marriage can be rooted in survival and a false sense of protection—however harmful their expression. None of that erases the inhumanity of early marriage; it strips away childhood, can cause lifelong trauma, and keeps cycles of gender inequality in place. And it can only exist when girls' lives are deemed as lesser, their agency denied, their humanity stripped away—robbed of both choice and dignity. But hearing the stories behind these choices—or, more often, the lack of choices—I started to hold the tension between the harm and the intent. Families may impose early marriage, but a society that offers no alternatives shares the blame. I continue to despise early marriage, yet I am less quick to rage at the families who enforce it without first understanding the systems that may leave them few other paths.

Farah and her husband, Alaa, fled Syria's civil war in the dead of night. They hitchhiked their way to Jordan, squeezed into the backs of trucks, moving in silence under the cover of darkness. Within two days of arriving at their destination, Farah gave birth to their little girl in a country where they had no official status.

Like the majority of Syrian refugees, Farah's family resided not in a camp but in a city. Zarqa teemed with factories and derelict apartment blocks, dense with people and poverty. Before the war, Farah had worked as a nurse in a government-run hospital, while her husband practiced law. In Jordan, however, their degrees meant nothing. He found work tiling floors at construction sites, only to be arrested three times for working illegally. The next arrest could mean indefinite detention.

"Now my husband stays at home," Farah shared as we sat together at a long table in an empty classroom where she worked as a primary school teacher. "He's depressed. Afraid of being sent to the camps."

With Alaa trapped by fear, Farah became the family's primary provider, securing a job at a school for Syrian and Jordanian children. But working outside the home came with its own risks. Zarqa's streets were notorious for crime, and for women, they were especially dangerous. In 2014, only one in ten Jordanian women worked outside the home. Part of the challenge was that simply being a woman in public invited scrutiny, suspicion, and, often, harassment. Women unescorted by a male family member were seen as sexually available, their presence alone interpreted as an invitation.

As part of my research, I ran focus groups on gender and employment. In one session, I sat with twelve Jordanian men between the ages of sixteen and twenty-four. I started with what I thought was a straightforward question: "Is it more difficult for women to find work?"

The answer came instantly: "No."

"If anything, it's easier for them," one male youth observed.

Another chimed in, "Women just flirt with the manager and get the job." The others nodded, scowling in agreement.

I'd expected them to say something along the lines of, *Women don't want to work—they'd rather get married and stay home.* As a researcher, my role wasn't to challenge or correct; it was to listen without judgment and probe. Still, I felt a jolt of disbelief.

In their minds, women weren't struggling to find work; they were manipulating their way into it. Any woman who had a job, they assumed, hadn't earned it through skill or effort but through seduction or favors. The idea that she might simply be qualified never crossed their minds. For some, it became a rationale for putting women "in their place," often through verbal abuse, social shaming, or sexual assault.

As I sat there listening to the conversation, my mind drifted back to Texas, where I grew up. My mom used to drag my sisters and me to Indian parties; I'd hover by the dining table, mostly for the food. The men would stand around with plates in hand, laughing loudly, debating politics and culture. There was a certain entitlement in their voices, as if they were the main characters in a show only they could star in. When little girls ran past the table, the men would scold them, "Go help in the kitchen," or "Stay quiet, don't make a scene." Then a group of boys would sprint by, grabbing food on their way to play volleyball outside. Not a word was said to them. Those moments seemed ordinary at the time. They taught me that power often sounds like certainty, and that patriarchy doesn't always shout; sometimes, it just takes the microphone.

Sitting with Farah in Jordan didn't feel all that different. The place had changed, but the pattern was the same, the instinct to tie women's freedom to male pride, control, and shame. Farah was caught in the middle of it, navigating a world where simply being outside her home could spark judgment, hostility, even violence. But her hardest battles weren't on the streets or at work. They were at home.

Her husband could not control her movements or her financial independence, which turned his anger into violence. When Farah started earning an income, it upended the traditional order at home. Alaa, unable to provide for or protect his family, saw his sense of manhood slip away. His frustration hardened into resentment; his pride twisted into suspicion. He began to question her every move—who was she with outside the home; why had she come home late?

"He'll hit me whether I have money or not," Farah said, meeting my eyes without flinching. "I'd rather have money." Her voice carried no anger, no self-pity.

Even the most determined person can't overcome the obstacles to finding safe, sustainable work without confronting the systems that keep them out. Legal restrictions, social bias, and exclusionary policies still block refugee women from access to livelihoods, protection, and dignity.

Displaced women can't build a plan B on their own. A viable future requires more than short-term aid; it demands legal rights, economic opportunity, and safe spaces to work and live. It means building communities that welcome and governments that include.

Years after I first met Aamina, we reconnected in Nairobi. I found a woman transformed. With a $250 loan from Grace's church group, she had expanded her injera business and moved her family into a small apartment with a concrete floor. She'd even bought a TV and a fridge. Grace, once her helper, had become her business partner, and together they hired a delivery driver so they could sell to hotels and restaurants farther afield. Her sons were finally back in school. The risks of street vending hadn't vanished, but now Aamina could plan for them.

I couldn't help but wonder: How much more could women like Aamina do if given real stability and inclusion? Because when displaced women are given the chance to build, they don't just get by—they create, they lead, and they lift entire communities.

2

Everyday Risk

Each person goes through life making everyday choices to keep themselves safe—often without even noticing. Harassment, theft, and other risks are part of everyone's experience; they don't care where you are, who you're with, or how you travel. Still, you probably notice that some places feel riskier than others, and some decisions carry more weight for your physical, emotional, or mental well-being. These choices, big or small, shape how you move through the world.

Try this exercise: Take a minute and write down all the things you do in your day-to-day life to stay safe.

The first time I tried this exercise, I was standing in front of a room of about forty practitioners working in the refugee camps across Ethiopia, along the Somali and Eritrean borders. Some had spent years in this work; others were new but eager.

As I offered instructions, I watched the room shift slightly, pens uncapped, eyes narrowed in thought. On one side of the room, the women were already writing. They listed things like:

- “I text a friend the license plate when I get into a taxi.”
- “I pretend to be on a phone call when I feel someone behind me.”
- “I avoid wearing certain clothes when walking alone.”
- “I carry my keys between my fingers.”
- “I cross the street to avoid groups of men.”
- “I wear a fake wedding ring.”

Their responses came fast, familiar, specific. Many women glanced at each other, nodding: This was their normal.

Meanwhile, across the room, the men hesitated. A few fidgeted with their pens. Some glanced around, unsure. One eventually offered out loud, “I guess . . . I work out. In case there’s a fight or something.” A few chuckled in response. Another wrote down something vague about being aware of his surroundings. For most of them, though, the paper in front of them stayed blank.

I didn’t rush to explain. I let the silence sit for a beat longer than it was comfortable. Then I asked, “What do you notice?”

This was when it clicked. You could see it in their faces, the men suddenly realizing they’d never had to think about these things; the women realizing how much they thought about them.

That moment is why I do this exercise. Because in the clearest, most undeniable way, it reveals a hard truth: Discrimination and risk for women aren't just things that happen "over there" or "to others." They're constant. They're everywhere. They cut across income, geography, and job title. Even in rooms like that one in Ethiopia, full of committed professionals, the exercise showed how invisible and normalized that disparity has become.

And that's the point I drive home next. If we, people who are designing or delivering aid programs, don't see these hidden layers of risk, we miss the full picture. My goal is to help aid workers integrate protection strategies into their programs so that female participants don't have to carry this burden alone; so that safety doesn't depend solely on personal vigilance, but becomes something we build into systems, services, and everyday practice.

The Jeep bounced and jolted along a dirt road, its white body emblazoned with the blue UNHCR logo. In spring 2012, my colleagues and I cut across the water-starved plains of eastern Ethiopia, bound for Sheder camp, home to 11,500 Somalis who had fled the unrelenting grip of civil war. Linkin Park thumped through my headphones, a steady pulse as I stared out at the passing landscape: scorched earth, spindly acacias, camels trudging in a slow, solemn procession, and, far off in the haze of heat, a mirage of wigwam-shaped huts rising into view.

My black Converse shoes were streaked with dust from the road as I stepped out of the Jeep and into the camp's checkpoint. Armed guards scrutinized every movement;

hand-scrawled logs were consulted, then double-checked, their ink smudged and faded from repeated use. I handed over my papers, and an officer took them with slow, deliberate precision. Names were called, signatures compared, stamps pressed, then pressed again. The whole procedure moved with the clunkiness of authority, slow, meticulous, and unyielding. The Ethiopian government's presence was a reminder that we were visitors on borrowed land, tolerated and watched.

The air shifted the instant I pushed open the door of the school classroom: cooler, quieter, electric with energy. Twenty girls, ages ten to sixteen, sat shoulder to shoulder, their faces flickering between shyness, suspicion, and curiosity. Fadia, twenty years old, round-faced and steady, acted as both guide and interpreter.

Whispers rose and fell behind hands, a few giggles snuffed out. One girl offered a tentative smile. I took a seat on a low wooden bench, introduced myself, and began my questions, starting with simple ones—daily life, chores, school—before moving into risk and resilience: how they earned money, whom they turned to for help, what they avoided and why. In that room, the rigid authority of the administration melted into the eager, searching eyes of the girls, a distinct contrast.

Their answers came in fragments and laughter, in long pauses and knowing looks exchanged between friends. Gradually, a picture began to form of their lives. Harm didn't announce itself; it crept in quietly, steadily, shaping the edges of girlhood. They confronted a wall of expectations: to leave school early, to marry young, to take up domestic work in the nearby town. And yet, each girl shared a desire to stay in school, to build a future of their own making.

They wanted to choose their partners and their jobs. One girl dreamed of becoming a doctor, another a physicist.

When it was their turn to ask me questions, all they wanted to know was if I was married.

Yes, came my answer.

"Was it a marriage for love?"

I nodded, which sparked another round of giggles. In that moment, I was reminded that beneath it all, across borders, systems, and circumstances, they were just teenage girls, dreaming of romance.

As Fadia and I made our way back to the Jeep, she paused. "Wait," she said softly, eyes scanning the space around us. Then she pulled me aside, out of earshot. Her voice dropped to a whisper. Something in her expression had shifted. She was no longer the bright-eyed guide from earlier, but someone holding something heavy.

"It happened two nights ago," she began. She had been asleep in her shelter when a man entered. She was crying now, her voice trembling, breaths uneven. "He held me down," she said, eyes fixed on me. "Shoved his fist in my mouth so no one would hear." The words landed hard. All of a sudden, the air felt thick, my chest tight, the heat making it hard to breathe.

She hadn't told anyone until now. Not because she didn't want to, but because she was afraid. Afraid of what her community might say, of the blame.

In conservative Somali culture, rape has long been seen as taboo and is rarely spoken of. When it is discussed, it's often framed as a deplorable, but ultimately uncontrollable act by a man under the influence of desire, alcohol, or anger. The old adage: Boys will be boys.

If and when it happens, a girl is rarely centered in the

experience or in the aftermath. Instead of being treated or protected, she might be forced to marry her assailant to preserve family honor. Or a settlement, financial or otherwise, might be quietly arranged between families. Through it all, the girl is often left carrying the weight of it, emotionally, socially, and physically, marked as impure, damaged.

I'd seen this same blame before. In Houston, the warmth of our old-fashioned Indian community evaporated after my mother divorced. The unspoken verdict: She hadn't done enough to keep the marriage together. It didn't matter what pain had lurked behind our front door. In the community's eyes, the responsibility fell entirely on my mother. Friends vanished. Invitations stopped coming. Neighbors who once dropped off food now averted their eyes. The isolation was swift and precise.

The one health clinic in Sheder camp was a single concrete room with two narrow beds and one nurse who seemed to do everything at once—doctor, midwife, counselor, record keeper. Supplies were stacked neatly in the corner, an order born from scarcity. Refugees and locals lined up on the benches outside, waiting under the hard sun.

Fadia knew that if she went to the clinic, she could receive care, but the nurse, a man, was required to report the case to the police. Whether she consented or not, an investigation would begin. Her secret would not stay hers for long.

In the end, she asked me for one thing: Could I help her get a door that locked? Something solid to replace the thin sheet of fabric that barely shielded her at night. That was all, not justice, just a way to feel safe again.

I thought helping Fadia would be simple. It felt obvious: She needed protection and giving it to her was the right thing to do. But it didn't take long for me to realize it wouldn't be so straightforward. Even a small change like swapping out the flimsy curtain for a solid, lockable door carried its own kind of danger. It could draw attention and raise questions. People might wonder why *she* should get special treatment, why *she* was being favored. And in a place where rumors move faster than sand, that kind of attention could be dangerous. It could mark her as a survivor, and with that would come judgment and isolation, or resentment and backlash.

A simple gesture of care could create more harm than good. I began to understand that sometimes protection isn't just about what you give; it's about how you offer it. In the end, Fadia was relocated to a safer part of the camp, where newer shelters had already been built, this time with doors.

This reminded me how different my own experience had been. As an undergrad at the University of Texas at Austin, I heard a male friend boast about having snuck into one of the administration offices to dig through student records and find out where a girl he liked lived. He saw the act as bold; I saw it as stalking. Horrified, I reported him immediately. But then, I didn't rely on him for my survival. I wasn't trapped in a web of social or economic dependence. For Fadia nothing was ever clear-cut. Survival wasn't just about food and shelter; it was about navigating a minefield of social codes, unspoken rules, and the very real fear of losing the little community and protection they offered.

If this is the reality that refugee women must navigate, limited choices and minimal support, how can we expand their options and strengthen their existing coping mechanisms?

When a crisis breaks out, the United Nations steps in. Born in the aftermath of World War II and shaped by the Allied powers—Great Britain, the United States, and the Soviet Union—the UN was built to prevent future wars. Its mission is broad but rooted in one idea: collective responsibility. The UN works to protect human rights, foster social and economic progress, deliver humanitarian aid, and uphold international law through global cooperation. In 2025, it counted 193 member states, almost every recognized country in the world.

It has negotiated peace deals, brokered ceasefires, and opened humanitarian corridors. In 2023 alone, it helped deliver aid to 128 million people.[1] That included the Black Sea Grain Initiative, which shipped food from war-torn ports in Ukraine and quite literally staved off global hunger.

So, how does it actually work? Well, behind almost every major humanitarian response is a machine. Picture a film crew on a high-stakes shoot. Each person has a job: directing, lighting, sound, camera, set design. They have to work in perfect sync to tell the story. In humanitarian crises, the UN agencies operate in much the same way: with distinct responsibilities and a shared mission. For example, after the 2010 earthquake in Haiti, which killed over 200,000 people and displaced 1.5 million, various UN agencies rushed in to help. UNHCR set up shelters and handed out emergency aid kits. UNICEF created safe spaces for children, supplied hospitals, and made sure clean water reached communities. The United Nations Population Fund focused on women's health and provided medical supplies for pregnant women and survivors of sexual violence. And the World Food Programme delivered food. Together, they worked to put out the metaphorical fire.

Within that big coordination system, the Inter-Agency Standing Committee, I worked with a group called the Gender-Based Violence Area of Responsibility, or GBV AoR. Bit of a mouthful, I know. But at its core, our job was simple: to make sure that preventing or responding to gender-based violence wasn't treated as an afterthought. It had to be part of the humanitarian response from day one. Sometimes it really worked. At other times—when you're there on the ground, sitting with someone like Fadia, whose life has just been torn apart—you start to see the cracks in the foundation, how the response was never designed with her in mind.

The reality is that GBV isn't a side issue that shows up later; it's woven into every crisis. Whenever people are displaced, whether by war, disaster, or persecution, the risk of violence against women and girls doubles.[2] It happens in shelters, at water points, on the way to the toilet; in someone else's home or sometimes one's own. And it's not just physical or sexual violence; it can be economic and psychological, too. It's forced early marriages, denial of education to girls, and intimate partner violence. And all these forms of violence escalate during a crisis. Here is a sobering statistic: One in three conflict-affected women will endure physical or sexual violence in their lifetimes. In some crisis settings, more than 70 percent of women and girls experience violence.[3] You'd think that preventing and responding to violence against women would be a global funding priority. But you'd be wrong. Violence against women receives just 0.2 percent of global development funds[4] and a staggeringly low 0.1 percent of humanitarian aid.[5] When we don't think about protection at the onset of a crisis, we are actively putting people in harm's way.

At thirty-seven, I became cochair of the GBV AoR. This was at a moment when women everywhere were pushing back against the status quo. The 2017 Women's March had just swept across U.S. cities. Soon after, the #MeToo movement erupted globally. And in a way that felt personal, *Wonder Woman* hit cinemas. I couldn't help but smile, thinking back to my childhood, when I'd twirl around in the living room pretending to be her, gold cuffs and all.

By then, I had conducted research in a dozen conflicts, trained more than two hundred practitioners, and implemented dozens of projects whose economic programs were both sustainable and gender-inclusive. Most humanitarian efforts focus on responding to gender-based violence, offering reproductive care, legal support, and emergency shelters for survivors. All critical, of course, but I wanted to stop the violence *before* it happened.

Here is how it works. Member organizations within the GBV AoR deploy teams of experts around the world to assess risks and offer guidance to host governments and humanitarian actors responding to a crisis. Sometimes the recommendations are simple and impactful, like installing well-lit, gender-segregated latrines in refugee camps to reduce the risk of sexual assault, but other times, the work requires more subtlety, like hosting weekly group discussions with couples on conflict resolution, gender roles, and communication to help reduce domestic violence that can occur in response to women's access to microloans.

My year as cochair taught me a lot, especially about the bureaucratic maze that is the UN system. I'll never forget my very first meeting. I was running five minutes late, stuck in an elevator that seemed determined to stop at every single floor. I could hear my husband's voice in my head, "If you're on time, you're late. If you're early, you're on time."

I anxiously stuffed a piece of Lindt dark chocolate into my mouth, waiting for the elevator doors to open. The meeting was held in a windowless room that buzzed with tension. I squeezed around the oversize conference table and slipped into the nearest open seat, trying to catch my breath. Within moments, I was swept into the choreography of interagency politics, an intricate, invisible dance that felt like stumbling into the mating ritual of a bird of paradise: all flair, display, and careful posturing. Each organization was politely snatching opportunities from the hands of others, puffing up its feathers for funders.

Before long, the conversation spiraled into a long, winding debate over who should update the Guidelines for Integrating Gender-Based Violence in Humanitarian Action. UNFPA had authored the original version back in 2005, so naturally, they argued, the responsibility should fall to them. But wait, UN Women hadn't existed back then; since that entity's creation in 2010, hadn't gender-based violence prevention become *their* mandate? Those in the room circled around these arguments, politely firm, diplomatically tense. In the end, it wasn't mandate that settled it. It was money. UNICEF would take the lead. Simply put, they could mobilize the necessary funding the fastest.

Inside the United Nations, securing funding depended on proving progress. But progress, in this context, wasn't measured by reduced violence, or more women with economic independence, or improved school retention rates for girls. It was measured in checked boxes: number of assessments conducted (check), number of refugees trained (check). And while training and assessments have their place, they don't in and of themselves keep women safe or protect their rights. The humanitarian system is addicted to measuring *process* over *impact*. Counting program participants is easy. It's tangible, trackable, and fits neatly into the one-year funding cycles that drive so much of the aid world. But the real work—changing harmful social norms, strengthening local protection systems, creating conditions that actually reduce violence—is more difficult to measure and takes time. And time isn't something donors, politicians, or the public like to fund.

Even worse, a huge portion of resources never makes it to the front lines. Out of all humanitarian funding in 2017–2023, only about 8.4 percent reached local governments, grassroots organizations, and community-based groups—those people best positioned to help.[6]

Observing this is like watching a house burn down while everyone argues over what color to repaint it. The scale of the emergency is undeniable, but the response remains painfully out of step. Is it really any surprise that Fadia had almost no expectations of protection from the very system meant to safeguard her?

The good news is that there is hope and, as it usually goes, it can be found in people. At the heart of the United Nations are thousands of aid workers who genuinely care, who show up, day after day, despite the constraints, because they believe in the safety, dignity, and futures of displaced people. With that in mind, the question that emerges isn't if the UN system can change. The question is how should it confront refugee women's protection head-on?

My time at the AoR helped me arrive at that question, but I had searched for the answer much earlier, between 2009 and 2012, when I served as senior livelihoods officer at the

Women's Refugee Commission. Those years were spent in the field, conducting research, developing tools, and training humanitarians on how to protect women while women earned a living. Because the truth is, economic empowerment can open doors, but without protection, it almost always carries risk.

Women typically adopt one of four strategies to manage the risks they face:

1. **Avoidance**—This strategy involves steering clear of potential dangers altogether. Women may change their daily travel routes, refuse certain job opportunities, or work from home to stay safe. In the Republic of Armenia, for example, according to a 2023 study by the Women's Resource Center, 95 percent of sexual harassment occurs in the workplace. Ninety-nine percent of these incidents go unreported to police, leading 56 percent of these women to resign from their jobs instead.[7]

2. **Containment**—This means actively managing and mitigating a threat to minimize its impact. Women may travel and sell goods in groups, bribe local police for protection, or accept lower wages to avoid conflict. In Nairobi, for example, police routinely stop refugees and demand national identity cards, which refugees don't have. Instead, they carry UNHCR-issued protection letters, which police often ignore or destroy, then they threaten arrest. To contain this risk, Somali refugees pay on average eleven dollars a month in bribes to avoid detention.[8] The goal of containment isn't to eliminate a threat; it's to make it manageable.

3. **Acceptance**—In some cases, women recognize that certain risks are unavoidable, and they choose not to take direct action against them. This might include exchanging sexual favors for employment, education, or aid or working in the informal sector, which can expose them to exploitation or legal consequences. More than half the world's refugees live in countries where their right to work is severely restricted, forcing many into unsafe labor conditions. In Lebanon, for example, when the government stopped allowing Syrian adults to register as refugees, it became nearly impossible for them to get work permits. The result? Families accepted child labor as a survival strategy, which led to the shocking reality that up to 60 percent of Syrian refugee children in Lebanon were working in 2017.[9] Instead of mitigating the threat, families braced for its consequences.

4. **Resistance**—Some women and communities take a stand against perpetrators, organizing self-defense groups or negotiating protection from authorities. In refugee camps, firewood collection is a particularly dangerous task for women, who often travel long distances through isolated areas, exposed to sexual assault by men from nearby villages. In Tanzania's Nyarugusu camp, an average of four sexual assaults per week occur during firewood collection.[10] But in 2016 women in the camp organized. They successfully petitioned African Union peacekeepers to escort them, significantly reducing the risk of attack.

Like the women of Nyarugusu, most refugee women don't passively accept risk. They strategize around it, balancing the need to earn an income with the dangers that come with it. Women and girls in crisis settings are not passive victims. They are active experts in their own safety. They can identify the threats they face, suggest strategies to manage them, and guide humanitarian practitioners on how to reduce their exposure to harm. The question is: Are we listening?

In 2008, I stepped into the Egyptian Sudanese Development Center, a modest building on a dusty street in Arba wy Nuss. The place was small, tucked between concrete buildings the color of sand, so unassuming you'd miss it if you blinked. Inside, the air smelled faintly of tea and the afternoon heat. A handful of plastic chairs, posters peeling off the wall, and a desk stacked with forms filled the room. The center offered training for Sudanese refugees and helped place them in domestic work—one of the few jobs available, though not legally. Domestic service was low-paying, hidden behind closed doors, and entirely unregulated. Power tilted dangerously in one direction. Paychecks went missing, employers shouted or leered, and sometimes the doors locked behind them.

The director, a quiet man with soft eyes, poured tea into chipped cups as he told me a story.

"There was a group of women," he started. "Sudanese refugees, all working in private homes. One day, they came to me, not angry, not crying, just tired. They asked if someone from the center could go with them to their jobs."

He stirred his tea slowly, the spoon tapping the glass as faint sounds of traffic drifted in from the open window. "Some had been harassed. Others . . . worse."

The director went on: The center began sending escorts, collecting employer details, noting wages, even drawing up informal codes of conduct. None of it carried legal weight, but it sent a clear, quiet message: *These women are not alone*. I thought of myself years earlier, walking home alone from the Metro in DC, pretending to be on the phone, proof that someone, somewhere was paying attention.

The afternoon light shifted as a woman entered the room at the center. Shaza was slim, composed, her eyes steady but weary. Her hands told her story, cracked from bleach, calloused from endless scrubbing, nails cut short. In the corner, her five-year-old daughter played on the floor, tenderly fixing her doll's tattered dress and matted hair, a small act of care in a world that offered little softness.

Shaza moved to Ard El Lewa, a crowded Sudanese neighborhood, after her husband had been killed in the street, stabbed by Egyptian men, who had chased him yelling racist slurs. Racism shadowed every errand, every bus ride, every knock on a neighbor's door. "They throw trash at us," she said. "They call us names; they throw stones. One man hurled a wooden plank with nails at my daughter."

It was safer, she explained, to live among other Sudanese. She shared a one-room flat with another family. The walls were thin, privacy thinner. "After rent and school fees," she told me, "I have maybe one hundred and fifty pounds [twenty-seven U.S. dollars at the time] left for food [for the month]. That is why we share flats. But when others have [male] relatives come to stay, it isn't safe."

In Cairo, power had an odd calculus. The moment a refugee woman began to earn, she also began to be at risk. A paycheck could buy independence or invite exposure. Behind the closed doors of middle-class apartments, Sudanese women scrubbed floors and ironed shirts, but wages vanished, hands wandered, and safety proved a fragile fiction.

Refugee women from Somalia, Ethiopia, and Eritrea all faced the same impossible arithmetic, survival at the cost of safety. And yet, even in the most broken systems, change can start with the smallest acts: a list of names, a promise to check in, a shared understanding that no one should have to survive alone.

When I think about safety now, I don't picture locked doors or bright streetlights. I think about people. Safety, I've come to realize, isn't just a physical state; it's a social one. It lives in the strength of our relationships, knowing who to call if I lose my job, need a place to crash, or can't pay a bill. It's my family, my best friend, maybe even a city program designed to catch me before I hit the ground. Just knowing that web exists, even if I never have to use it, gives me a steady kind of confidence.

Everyone's safety net looks different. Maybe it's a church group that drops off meals, a neighbor who checks in, or a local organization that helps cover rent. What matters isn't the size of the network, but the reliability of its ties. One steady connection can offer more protection than a dozen polite acquaintances.

We don't usually talk about social networks as safety systems, but they are. They decide how hard we fall, how long we stay down, and how fast we rise back up. For refugees, they offer job leads, housing recommendations, credit, and information.

In Johannesburg, Somali shopkeepers buy goods in bulk together and sell surplus to one another at discounted rates. In Kampala, Congolese refugees run awareness campaigns warning newcomers about the dangers of street vending, where police crackdowns can turn violent. For people locked out of official government services, these networks are a lifeline.

But not all networks are the same. Refugees often rely on two kinds of connections: *bonding networks*, those built within their own communities and *bridging networks*, the harder-to-reach ties that connect them to host communities or people with more resources. Bonding networks make the early days easier. Those who arrive in a new city with family or friends already there find their footing faster than those who land alone. But these same networks can also become limiting. When everyone you know is doing the same kind of work, your options narrow. Vietnamese refugees in the United States often find themselves clustered in nail salons; Eritrean men in cities like Nairobi or Tel Aviv frequently end up as night guards. These jobs offer stability, but they can also box people in, keeping them on the margins of the economies they help sustain.

For women, these limits are often even sharper. Gender norms shape nearly every aspect of life, where women can go, whom they can talk to, and whether they can work at all. When you enter a community that holds strict ideas about women's roles, your choices narrow to fit those expectations. In some Somali communities, for example, girls are expected to stay home instead of going to school, and women are discouraged from working outside the household. That kind of social pressure can make it nearly impossible to step beyond the boundaries of your community, even when you want to. For refugee women, the cost of defying these norms can be isolation, judgment, or even danger. So many end up trapped in a cycle of dependence, not because they lack ambition, but because the networks around them demand compliance in exchange for belonging.

These same cultural expectations make it even harder for women to meet others in public. Women are often more socially isolated than men, their movement limited by both custom and caution. In many places, a woman alone in public draws unwanted attention; she is seen as vulnerable, or worse, as inviting it. Safety concerns and social judgment combine to keep women indoors, where opportunities to build relationships or seek support shrink to almost nothing. Without safe public spaces, even simple acts, attending a meeting, sharing information, finding work, making a friend, become difficult.

It was a Wednesday evening in Nairobi, two years after my first visit, when I found myself once again with Grace. Aamina stayed behind to watch the boys and tend to the injera, while Grace and I caught a matatu across town to her church.

The building rose from the red dust, a simple wooden frame, an earthen floor, rows of plastic chairs. The air inside was cool, sliced by shafts of late sunlight slipping through the gaps between the wooden planks of the wall. As the service began, the choir lifted their voices, rich and full, hands clapping in rhythm. Grace sang too, her face bright with joy. The pastor spoke, and from every corner came the soft, rolling echo of *Amen*.

When the service ended, the crowd thinned, but the energy lingered. Fifteen women stayed behind, dragging their chairs into a circle at the front of the church. Someone passed around a tin cup of sweet tea.

Grace introduced me quietly. "We are all sellers," she said, and the women nodded. Most had spent years hawking goods on the streets—soap, fruit, secondhand clothes—earning just enough to survive. They were street-smart; they knew when to run, when to hide, which officers demanded bribes and which ones turned a blind eye.

Fridays were the worst, they said. Police patrols swept through the markets like storms, confiscating goods and demanding payment. So, they made a rule: no selling on Fridays. To cover the cost of a bribe, they could borrow small sums from this savings group, the same one that had helped Aamina start her injera business.

Now, one by one, each woman pulled a few folded notes from her purse, one dollar here, two there, and deposited them into a metal lockbox held in the lap of the elected secretary. Each contribution was met with applause and with laughter.

I'd heard them called *djanggi* in Cameroon, *tanda* in Mexico, *chits* in India. Different names, same beat: women pooling small amounts to build something more secure and steady. The rules were simple enough, put money in regularly, take a loan when you must (based on agreed-upon conditions), pay it back, and when the year ends, everyone shares in the savings and profits. This system provides an accessible and flexible source of financing, particularly benefiting women, who often save in small amounts, take modest loans, and use the funds to stabilize household food and income.

But the real power wasn't in the money; it was in the gathering. In a place where formal banks saw refugees, the ultra-poor, and women as risks too great to touch, this circle of women had built their own institution, one founded on trust and sustained by accountability. For Grace, the savings group offered protection. The women became each other's safety net, guarding children, swapping information, and accompanying one another through the city's crowded streets, a shield against unwanted attention.

Still, for those with husbands, there were challenges to navigate. "Not consulting the man," Grace explained, "is disrespectful. It can cause fights." The women nodded. One woman described hiding her earnings in a flour tin. Another said she always asked permission before attending the meetings.

Outside, the night deepened. I watched as they stepped out into the dark.

If humanitarian organizations truly want to protect refugee women, they must invest in the networks these women have already built. Grace, Fadia, and Aamina do not have to navigate danger and uncertainty alone.

Too often, the solutions women create themselves are overlooked. Listening to them, supporting their strategies, and providing real options can transform small acts into powerful safeguards. A peer escort to a job, a simple code of conduct, a two-dollar contribution to a savings group, each choice becomes a foothold, a way to rise. And time and again, refugee women show that with trust, solidarity, and a little support, they will rise.

3

The Bootstrap Myth

For Doris, the price of success had always been high.

In Nigeria, she was a force. A respected lawyer, the founder of a legal aid clinic that had secured the release of more than two hundred wrongfully detained women. She fought tirelessly to protect widows from losing their homes, held domestic abusers accountable, and challenged forced marriages. Her mission was to build a society where a person's rights and livelihood were determined not by their gender but by their humanity.

Doris wasn't just practicing law; she was challenging deeply ingrained norms. As a single mother, she was dismantling kinship structures and generational beliefs that treated women as inferior to men. She was raising a new generation that would teach their sons to respect women and their daughters to know their worth.

The world noticed. In 2013, her nonprofit gained "special consultative status" with the Economic and Social Council of the United Nations. But her growing international recognition came at a cost. By exposing corruption in the legal system, she became a target. In 2018, she was abducted, tortured, and left for dead.

Miraculously, she survived. Fleeing to the United States with nothing but the clothes on her back, her two children, and her elderly mother, she arrived in Chicago with no suitcase or keepsakes, just a single desperate hope: to rebuild.

It was not an easy transition. Her qualifications and work experience meant little. Three hundred job applications later, she had no offers in law or administration. With no money coming in, Doris took what jobs she could find: low-wage, unskilled, and easy to get. Every night, she left her cramped one-bedroom apartment, boarded a bus, and spent ninety minutes crossing the city. Then came a twelve-hour shift on the factory floor, repeating the same motions, hour after hour. It was steady work, but it wasn't enough to climb out of poverty. She felt it every day. In 2019, after a year of backbreaking labor, she told me, "I hardly see my children. I feel like I'm letting them down, despite having so much more to offer." In Nigeria, she was a force for justice. In Chicago, she was just another Black woman from a poor African country. No one saw her as a lawyer, an advocate, or a leader. She missed the breakfast table with her kids, volunteering at church, the small joy of getting her nails painted.

Much of the world insists that poverty is a choice, that grit and determination alone can lift a person out of hardship. It's a belief that stretches back nearly two centuries, from the industrial boom to the Protestant work ethic: the notion that hard work, self-discipline, and frugality were signs of moral worth. It reminds us that we only have ourselves to blame as wealth, the sign of God's blessing, is achieved by overcoming personal, spiritual, and moral deficits. Over time, that idea hardened into one of America's most enduring myths, the belief that anyone can succeed through sheer determination, and conversely we deserve our poverty when it happens. The "bootstrap" idea turned work into a kind of salvation, wealth into virtue, and poverty into personal failure. In doing so, it masked the real forces that determine success—access to resources, laws and services, and community acceptance—and made it easier for societies to overlook the structural inequalities that keep millions trapped in cycles of deprivation.

That mindset still dominates today. A 2020 Pew Research Center survey[1] found that 65 percent of Americans—across income levels, gender, and ethnicities—believe poverty stems from individual shortcomings. By that logic, Doris's struggle wasn't the result of structural barriers; it was her own fault.

And yet, more than half[2] of the 15 million women living in poverty in the United States work full-time.[3] Hard work alone cannot close wage gaps, erase discrimination, or overcome laws that block women from credit, property, or inheritance. You can't pull yourself up by the bootstraps if you were never given boots. And still, society tells women like Doris: *Work harder, and you'll rise.* For women, hard work is not a ladder, it's a treadmill.

My mother was not a refugee, but she was one of these women, grinding away in multiple jobs, sacrificing everything for the chance to give her children a better life. In 1973, she left India for an arranged marriage, eventually settling in Texas to raise four daughters. Following a divorce, she made a decision that would define the rest of her life: She chose to raise us on her own. Her parents begged her to come back to India, to return to the safety of home, free childcare, a supportive community. But my mother refused. She stayed because she wanted us to have a life in which our choices weren't dictated by tradition, in which we would be free to decide our own futures in marriage, education, and career. That meant she was on her own.

She joined the ranks of the educated poor, the 2.1 million immigrants, refugees, and asylees who leave behind their credentials for a chance at a better or safer future.[4] Despite holding a master's degree in English literature from Panjab University, one of India's most prestigious institutions, she struggled to find a professional job. Her qualifications were deemed equivalent to a U.S. bachelor's degree, not a master's. So, she pivoted, applying to high school teaching jobs, hoping to match her work schedule to our academic ones, but HR departments across Texas rejected her. "You can't teach English literature in America as a foreigner," they told her.

Her response was swift, biting, and true: "I speak the Queen's English."

It didn't matter.

So, she did what millions of other women in her position do: She hustled. By day, she was a bank teller. By night, she cashed out the registers at Sears. There was no one else to watch us, so my sisters and I spent hours sitting on the dingy beige carpeting of the store, waiting for her shift to end. On weekends, our family of five piled into a battered station wagon to peddle Avon products door-to-door. (For low-income families scraping by on multiple jobs, this is what childcare looks like.)

My mother worked and worked and worked. But it was never enough.

Two-thirds of adults living in poverty in the United States have jobs. They work an average of 1.7 jobs just to survive.

Among low-income families, 83 percent of children have at least one working parent, and nearly 60 percent have a parent working full-time, year-round.[5]

Women outwork men in every way that doesn't count on a paycheck.

They take on the invisible labor, the cooking, the cleaning, the child-rearing, the care of elderly parents. And on top of work and family responsibilities, they bear another unseen burden: the emotional labor of holding their communities together. They nurse sick parents. They organize school activities. They check in on neighbors, plan celebrations, run food drives, and sustain faith communities. And they do it all without recognition, without pay, without rest. In sub-Saharan Africa, women spend twelve to thirteen more hours per week in agricultural labor than men.[6] In China and South Korea, they devote three times as many hours as men to care-related work.[7] Moving wider, globally, women shoulder double the unpaid care work, which amounts to an annual $10.8 trillion in unremunerated value—the fair market value of domestic tasks.[8] That means, on average, women work an extra month per year compared to men for nothing.[9] Climbing the economic ladder gets a lot more difficult when you're carrying triple the load with no support.

Make no mistake: This has consequences. Women caregivers suffer higher rates of stress, anxiety, and depression.[10] Their life satisfaction is lower than men's. They die younger. And because their labor is unpaid or underpaid, the idea of "working your way up" is nothing more than a myth of meritocracy.

The responsibility of caregiving—regularly looking after a child or a sick, elderly, or disabled person—currently sets women on a fundamentally different path from men. It shapes opportunity, advancement, and even the experience of work itself, yet society rarely acknowledges it. The very act of caregiving, essential to the survival of families and economies alike, is treated as a personal choice rather than a public good.

In the United States, that neglect carries a steep price. Childcare costs are crushing: 40 percent of parents go into debt[11] to afford it, spending on average 27 percent of their income on it. In 2023, that meant more than $18,000 per child, about $1,500 a month.[12] The consequences ripple outward. Mothers quit jobs, reduce hours, or delay returning to work, costing the U.S. economy an estimated $122 billion each year[13] in lost productivity. Over a lifetime, those reduced hours translate to nearly $300,000 in lost retirement savings for mothers. And the burden falls unevenly: 17 percent of Black mothers and 16 percent of Latine mothers[14] quit, change, or turn down jobs due to childcare challenges, compared with 10 percent of white families. Even the caregivers themselves, most of them women of color, barely survive on poverty wages. Nearly 70 percent of childcare workers cannot afford basic necessities like food and utilities.[15]

I felt this difference the moment I became a mother. Returning to work after my first child, I was terrified. How could I be both a high-performing professional and a fully present, loving mom? The fear of failing on both fronts gnawed at me. Daycare brought its own chaos, endless illnesses, strict pickup times, and the quiet ache of missing another class celebration while sitting at my desk. Work trips were worse; I'd leave for two weeks at a time. My husband worked long hours, so my mother would fly in to help. We cobbled it all together the best we could, but the daily juggling and exhaustion were relentless. I kept my job, but it came at the cost of career growth.

When I think about my mother working three jobs to keep us afloat, or about Doris escaping torture only to labor on a factory floor in Chicago, I see the same pattern repeating across generations. Their struggles were never about bad choices or a lack of effort. They worked harder than most people ever will, and still they were set up to hit a low-lying ceiling. Society continues to insist: *If you're struggling, it's your fault. If only you had worked a little harder. If only you had made better choices.*

But what if the choices were never real? What if the system was designed so that no matter how hard you worked, you would never get ahead?

In 2021, the first time I met Aisha, she was standing outside a job center in the Bronx, her coat too thin for the February wind. She had just moved out of a homeless shelter with her three sons and was searching for professional work. In Sudan, she had been a journalist, her voice steady and familiar on national radio and UN broadcasts, reporting on women's rights through the chaos of civil war, a war she would eventually flee. She carried a degree in business administration from Khartoum University, a quick mind, and a spine of steel.

After months of job rejection letters, Aisha retrained as a home health aide. Each morning began before dawn: two bus transfers, a long walk through the city still half asleep.

Her work was physical. She lifted, cleaned, fed, and comforted her elderly client, then did it all again. For $1,500 a month, every dollar counted. When one of her boys got sick, she faced a choice: lose a day's wages or leave him home alone. "I don't understand," she told me once, eyes defiant. "The woman at the shelter said this is a good job."

In some ways, the case manager at the homeless shelter wasn't wrong. In 2022, the United States spent an astonishing $132.9 billion on home healthcare,[16] double the amount the country spent on public transportation,[17] triple what it allocated to K–12 public schools,[18] and a jaw-dropping twenty-three times more than it invested in climate finance.[19] The demand for home health aides was booming. The industry was growing. And yet, one in five such aides lived in poverty.[20] Why? Because being a health aide was considered women's work, and women's labor, whether paid or unpaid, is chronically undervalued.

Look at the industries dominated by women: caregiving, teaching, administrative work. These jobs are essential; society depends on them. And yet, even when there's a labor shortage, wages stay low. Meanwhile, industries that employ more men tend to offer higher pay, better benefits, and greater prestige, regardless of the education or skills required.[21]

Take computer science. In the 1950s, coding was seen as clerical, something akin to typing, and therefore considered women's work. By the 1980s, computer programming shifted to a high-status, male-dominated field. Personal computers were marketed primarily to boys, media reinforced the image of the male geek, and hiring practices favored men. The result? Salaries skyrocketed, and the industry gained prestige.

Now flip the script. What happens when more women start entering a field? Pay drops.

Take park rangers and the camping industry. Back in the 1950s, it was mostly men doing the work. Now that it's majority women, the median hourly wage has fallen by 57 percent. When more women started working in biology, wages dropped 18 percent.[22] In design, they plummeted by a third.

It's not that women end up in low-wage jobs because they lack skills or because those jobs aren't in demand. *It's that these jobs pay less because women are doing them.* This is why the idea that simply giving women more skills will fix everything doesn't hold up. Getting the right degree and the right credential won't solve wealth disparity when the value of entire industries shrinks as soon as women become the majority of the workforce.

And it's not just gender. When you layer in race and immigration status, the financial penalties stack up. For every dollar a white man earns:

- White women earn 80 cents;
- Black women earn 63 cents;[23]
- Latine women earn 57 cents;[24] and
- Immigrant women earn just 53 cents.[25]

The inequity doesn't stop there. On average, a white high school dropout has more wealth than a Black college graduate. Immigrant women with master's degrees earn just 55 cents for every dollar earned by U.S.-born men. Over a lifetime, this gap can cost them up to $1.26 million compared to U.S.-born men.[26] While U.S.-born women gain nearly

$17,700 from earning a master's degree, immigrant women see only a $3,900 increase.

This is the reality refugee women walk into when they arrive in the United States. They aren't just fighting to survive as newcomers. They're navigating a deeply rigged system where their gender, race, and immigration status compound their lack of access to opportunity.

Administrative policies have long kept communities of color and immigrants from building wealth, and that tradition continues to this day. Take redlining, a government-sanctioned practice whose impacts still shape communities across the country. For decades, banks marked neighborhoods with large populations of Black, brown, and immigrant families as "high-risk" areas, effectively cutting them off from mainstream financial services like mortgages. Today, homes in formerly redlined neighborhoods are still valued 23 percent less than comparable homes in predominantly white areas. That gap represents $162 billion in lost wealth, enough to pay for 82 million four-year college degrees.[27]

Even after redlining was formally banned, it evolved into predatory lending practices that emerged in its place. With traditional credit still often denied to them, many Black, Latine, and immigrant borrowers were funneled into subprime loans, even when they qualified for better options. These loans came with usurious interest rates, hidden fees, balloon payments, and adjustable rates that spiked without warning. Worse, the loans were frequently structured to fail. Borrowers had little flexibility during times of hardship, foreclosure was fast-tracked, and lenders were often incentivized to foreclose rather than modify loans. These administrative and financial systems didn't just limit access; they actively extracted wealth from communities of color.

The racial and gender wealth gaps in America weren't accidents of history; they were engineered. They are the products of laws, labor practices, and social systems that have, for generations, denied women, immigrants, and communities of color the chance to build and transfer wealth.

So, it's no wonder Aisha was confused by her case manager's advice. Yes, there was demand for home health aides. Yes, it was "a good job" in the narrow sense that it offered steady hours. But the path it offered led nowhere new. She had done everything "right": earned a college degree, built a respected career, retrained, worked hard. And still, she was trapped in the same cycle of survival her mother had known in Sudan by a system that wasn't designed to reward effort.

At dawn, Khartoum woke slowly. The air was thick with dust and diesel, and the city hummed with the sound of vendors setting up for the day. Aisha's mother spread a woven mat on a cracked stretch of pavement, in front of rusted storefronts with fading Arabic signs. Around her, the street filled with color and movement, sellers stacking their vegetables, boys hawking sandals, women balancing baskets of flatbread on their heads. From a dented tin kettle, she poured steaming tea into five glass cups, rinsing each one in a bucket of murky water between customers.

She was a *sitat el shay*, a tea lady. It's honest work, but dangerous. She didn't have a vendor's permit, so every day she watched for the police. They came in trucks, loud and sudden, scattering vendors like startled birds. Sometimes they took her earnings. Sometimes they took her kettle. Sometimes they took her, calling her a prostitute.

Aisha's mother was one of millions uprooted by the tribal wars in South Sudan, an internally displaced person (IDP), meaning she was forced to flee her home but remained within her country's borders. Unlike refugees, IDPs do not cross an international boundary and therefore are not granted the formal legal protections and assistance that accompany refugee status. She was part of a global population of approximately 62.5 million IDPs, a figure that has grown to nearly twice the number of refugees worldwide.[28] She lived in a makeshift shack on the outskirts of Khartoum, part of a settlement that stretched for miles, where 2.5 million others shared her fate. She was illiterate, innumerate, and confined to the only labor market open to her: the informal economy, the global shadow workforce of vendors, cleaners, and caregivers. For women like her, it is both lifeline and cage: no labor protections, no benefits, no childcare, no advancement, and no income if they miss a day's work. Yet this is where most of the world's women labor.

She worked hard to ensure Aisha had legal rights, professional credentials, and a good education, everything she needed to enter the formal economy. And yet Aisha still found herself climbing the same steep hill her mother had faced before her.

When I ask myself, why was it so hard for my mother to thrive economically, the answer is simple. She was not failing; the system was failing her. When we stop pretending that individual effort alone can overcome systemic oppression, we begin to see women's lives differently. Change doesn't come from working harder; it comes from rewriting the rules. It starts with ensuring a living wage and job quality for all workers, especially in the lowest-paid jobs, where women are most concentrated. It means building robust social safety nets that include healthcare, sick leave, unemployment benefits, and paid parental leave. It means restructuring the informal sector so that women who sell food, clean homes, or sew clothes are guaranteed fair labor protections and collective bargaining rights.

4

Invisible Walls

In 1989, Kimberlé Crenshaw published her landmark article "Demarginalizing the Intersection of Race and Sex" in the *University of Chicago Legal Forum*. She was motivated by legal cases in which discrimination claims brought by Black women were dismissed because the harm could not be attributed solely to race or solely to gender. In response, Crenshaw introduced the concept of intersectionality, a framework that reveals how multiple systems of oppression, including racism, sexism, and classism, operate not in isolation but intersect. Intersectionality demonstrates that inequity cannot be understood or meaningfully addressed through a single-axis lens; it requires examining how intertwined structures of power shape lived experience.

From an intersectional research standpoint, displacement provides a vivid illustration of how such overlapping systems converge. Forced migration does not merely expose women to a new set of challenges; it places them at the intersection of immigration enforcement, racial hierarchy, economic marginalization, and gender subordination. Each of these structures functions on its own, yet together they generate forms of vulnerability that no single framework can fully explain.

When displaced women enter host societies that marginalize or criminalize them, they often do so without stabilizing buffers—community ties, economic resources, or familiarity with institutions—that help mitigate harm. A gender analysis alone would highlight sexism; a racial analysis would uncover discrimination; a migration review would point to legal precarity.

Across global contexts, one pattern remains striking: Gender oppression is a constant, a stable variable in an otherwise shifting landscape. This constancy might suggest the possibility of broad-based solidarity among all women. Yet decades of research reveal that solidarity is often undermined by the very hierarchies that intersectionality makes visible. Race, class, sexuality, and citizenship status create stratifications among women, determining whose safety is prioritized, whose voices are amplified, and who is left to navigate danger alone.

The result is not only fragmentation but *misrecognition*: the mistaken belief that one group's struggle is wholly separate from another's, rather than differentiated expressions of interconnected systems of power. Intersectionality shows that sexism never operates in isolation; it is filtered through other structures that shape its impact. Efforts to confront gender inequality that ignore these dimensions inevitably reproduce the exclusions they claim to challenge.

Research consistently demonstrates that when movements center only the experiences of the most socially protected women, the solutions they generate fail those at the margins. But when advocacy is informed by an intersectional understanding of power, the outcomes become more expansive, more just, and more sustainable.

For two summers of my childhood, I left Texas to stay with relatives in Chandigarh, India, including my aunt and uncle. My aunt married soon after finishing her college degree and settled into the life of a stay-at-home spouse. Her world revolved around managing the home, kids, and social events. Her influence remained tethered to the domestic sphere.

One scorching afternoon, when a snake charmer wandered into the neighborhood, we ran to her begging for money to watch him perform, and she gladly gave it. The man sat cross-legged on a faded cloth, placed a woven basket before him, and lifted a double-reeded pungi to his lips. As the music floated through the thick air, the basket's lid trembled, and a cobra slowly rose, swaying to the rhythm. It was magic.

Yet beneath that magic ran another current. As tender as my aunt could be with us, the way she spoke to the servants told a different story. She demanded perfection from them through relentless repetition of tasks. She controlled their appearance, dictated what they wore, how they styled their hair, even which soap they used. Mistakes were met with stern rebukes or a barrage of insults. Her behavior was likely a reflection of her own confinement by social rules: Deprived of broader avenues of power and dignity, she exerted what little authority she had over those less empowered.

That stark contrast revealed the invisible scaffolding of the hierarchy on which our communities rest, determining who holds power, rights, and access to opportunities. Our place within the structure shapes our interactions, molds our identities, and affects how we see ourselves and our value in the world.

Long before I was born, on the outskirts of Ambala Cantt, a city about 130 miles north of New Delhi, my mother spent her 1960s childhood in a British colonial home. The single-story residence featured ceilings of intricate woodwork, beneath which fans twirled in a perpetual, languid ballet. The fans' soft whirring mingled with the buzz of nature and birdsong that floated in through the windows, while the cool tile floors provided respite from the sultry heat. A wraparound veranda and lush, colorful gardens extended indoors, with walls painted in shades of light and dark blue, depicting Indian roller birds, creating what my mother recalls as a tranquil oasis.

Just a stone's throw from the home were the kitchen and servants' quarters—discreet, separate, yet indispensable to the daily rhythm of life. The servants came from India's lowest caste, the Sudra. The caste system has been in existence in India for three thousand years. Rooted in Hindu belief, it organizes society into four main groups with numerous subcastes. Whichever caste you are born into is believed to be based on karma, or how you lived your past life. On top, karma places Brahmans as priests and teachers, then Kshatriyas as rulers and soldiers, Vaishyas as merchants and traders, and, finally at the base, Sudras as laborers. Outside this social pyramid are the Dalits, deemed so impure that they are considered unworthy of a caste.

Dalits, historically labeled "untouchables," have endured marginalization in every aspect of social, economic, and cultural life, facing rampant discrimination and segregation.

They are relegated to the most demeaning tasks. In homes without indoor plumbing, they handle human waste, a job considered too impure for higher castes. A Dalit worker will discreetly use a back door to clean latrine pots, reinforcing their invisibility and the stigma of their duties. Dalit women in rural areas often work as scavengers.

Lakshmi was one of the Dalit cleaners in my mother's home. She was not allowed to enter the kitchen, touch utensils, or sit in a chair. Unlike other servants, she lived on the outskirts of town, in a segregated, sun-scorched complex of mud-walled houses. My mother was probably the only higher-caste person ever to visit Lakshmi's home, and she was harshly reprimanded by her mother for doing so. My mother described the house vividly: the baked bricks and corrugated metal roof that trapped the stifling heat, turning it into a sweltering enclosure; the floors, made of compacted earth, and coated with a thin layer of cow dung, a traditional disinfectant; and the rooms, sparse but functional. Simple wooden cots with woven jute or cotton ropes served as beds. Dalits like Lakshmi were barred from using communal resources like wells and temples, as their presence was believed to contaminate these places.

Despite the legal end of untouchability in 1950, ostracizing and demeaning practices continued. In 2021, one in three Dalits lived in what is called "multidimensional poverty," a designation that looks at markers of health and education in addition to standards of living.[1] Half of Dalit women could not read or write,[2] compared to less than one in four other Indian women.[3]

Activist Sujatha Gidla's 2017 memoir, *Ants Among Elephants*, describes growing up as a Dalit in New Delhi. Each morning, she would stuff her notebooks into a jute sack, which also served as her seat on the ground during class. Her family's meager earnings meant she had to start work at sixteen to fund her education and personal needs. At school, she kept her social status to herself. "If you are educated like me," she wrote, "you can either tell the truth and face ostracism, ridicule, harassment—even suicide, as happens regularly in universities. Or you can lie." In 2021, Dalits made up only 14 percent of university students[4] but accounted for nearly 60 percent[5] of 13,000 student suicides.[6] For Dalit women, sexual violence is alarmingly high. Upper-caste men commit 80 percent of the assaults. The perpetrators are often landlords or their agents or, at construction sites, contractors and their crews.[7]

Like social segregation, occupational segregation is not natural selection based on preference, but a system carefully engineered and maintained to signal who belongs where. And as with any caste system, the hierarchy branches inward, producing subcastes shaped by gender, class, origin. In Brazil, the racial order forged during colonial rule placed whites at the apex, mixed-race populations in the uneasy middle, and Afro-Brazilians and Indigenous communities at the base. Power sustained the structure by controlling access to land, rights, and economic mobility: Fertile agricultural holdings were reserved for whites, while Afro-Brazilians were funneled into informal labor with little chance of advancement.

The scaffolding has proven remarkably resilient. Today, Afro-Brazilians are twice as likely as their white counterparts to be poor. Those with advanced degrees earn significantly less.[8] This pattern echoes across Latin America. In 2014, poverty rates in Ecuador were 42 percent for Afro-descendants compared to 27 percent for non-Afro-descendants. In Peru, the figure was 21 percent versus 14 percent; and in Uruguay, 11 percent versus 4 percent.[9] The numbers differ by country, but the architecture is familiar.

Gender follows the same blueprint. Policymakers and employers have steered women toward work that is undervalued and underpaid—caregiving, clerical roles, piecework—while men are ushered into fields associated with authority and financial security, from engineering to finance.

Too often, even well-meaning humanitarian programs reinforce these lines. I've visited countless projects that proudly trained women in sewing, carpet weaving, and beading, skills that delivered scant income and no autonomy.

In many countries, national policies deepen the divide by tying women to a single employer, denying them legal permission to work, or leaving those in informal jobs without protection. Hierarchy, once constructed, learns how to protect itself.

It is one thing to describe such restrictions in policy terms; it is another to witness how they rearrange a life. Nwe Nwe was only nineteen when she met her future husband in the bustling streets of Yangon, Myanmar, also known as Burma. She had just started teaching school; he was a police officer. They were building a life together, dreaming quietly between lessons and night shifts, raising their three daughters, ages seven, eight, and ten. Their future felt steady, full of possibility.

Then came February 1, 2021. The morning air in Yangon felt the same as any other, until it didn't. The military had staged a coup, toppling the elected government. Streets became battlegrounds overnight. Soldiers with assault rifles patrolled every corner. Internet blackouts silenced voices. Friends vanished. Teachers, nurses, even teenagers, gone without warning. Four years after the coup, at least 6,000 people had been killed, nearly 20,000 arrested, and close to 3.5 million internally displaced.[10]

Fear wrapped itself around their lives. Nwe Nwe and her husband joined the Civil Disobedience Movement, striking and protesting peacefully. And then one day, her husband didn't come home. The military had taken him. Grief-stricken, Nwe Nwe knew she had to get her daughters to safety. They fled, traveling more than three hundred miles to cross into Thailand.

The refugee camp was grim, a permanent "temporary" holding ground for 130,000 Burmese who had fled before them, some as early as 1984.[11] But there was no work in the camp, no income, nothing to put food on the table. Desperation pushed her to a nearby village to borrow money from a friend. Thai police arrested her for leaving the camp, detained her for three days, and then dumped her on a riverbank near the Burmese border. She stumbled back to the camp, exhausted.

She realized she could not survive there, so they moved to Mae Sot, a city crowded with migrant workers from Myanmar, Laos, and Cambodia. Once she left the camp, she became an undocumented migrant, losing any legal protections she held as a refugee.

Factories lined the streets. Nwe Nwe found undocumented work in a garment factory. It was seven days a week, fifteen hours a day, in a small, filthy room that felt like a chicken coop. The minimum daily wage was ten dollars; she earned one to two dollars a day. She earned enough to feed her children, but her employer deducted pay for housing and medical care. If she complained, she would be replaced in an instant. Burmese factory workers like her lived paycheck to paycheck, trapped in debt, tied to their employers.

Nwe Nwe found herself shoulder to shoulder with other women in the garment factories of Mae Sot, refugees like her, alongside local Thai women who had been laboring in the same conditions. Thai women endured equally grueling hours, withheld wages, and unsafe conditions. Many labored sixty-plus hours a week, with few breaks and rampant physical abuse. Safety standards were ignored, health risks brushed aside. Both groups were trapped in systems that exploited women. Refugee women struggled with restrictive legal rights and almost no safety net. Local women fought to enforce the minimal protections they were legally entitled to.

Of course, the challenges and opportunities were never the same for all women; they shifted along lines of class, ethnicity, ability, and tribe. There was no single narrative of feminism in that factory, only overlapping realities shaped by where each woman stood in the social hierarchy. But my reflection is this: Solidarity begins when we make room for those varied realities, especially the ones forged at the bottom of that hierarchy.

Zuri was twenty-four, a single mother of three, and a refugee from the Democratic Republic of the Congo trying to build a new life in Wisconsin. When she first arrived in 2016, the world felt cold in more ways than one—the sharp Midwestern wind biting her skin, the language of her new home tangled on her tongue. A local resettlement agency helped her find a janitorial job and a small apartment, offering three months of support, just long enough to take a breath, but not enough to rebuild. In that narrow window, she had to learn English, enroll her children in school, and navigate a maze of welfare forms written in words she did not understand. Then, just like that, the caseworker was gone, and Zuri was on her own.

The apartment she shared with another single mother sat in a forgotten corner of Milwaukee, a place where the streets were lined with dilapidated houses, their exteriors faded and peeling from years of neglect. Unkempt yards were littered with debris and rusted appliances. Weeds pushed stubbornly through the pavement, and the few remaining shops were hidden behind metal grilles and defaced by graffiti. Inside, the toilet overflowed, the kitchen window was shattered, and cockroaches moved freely across the counters. When the landlord ignored her complaints, Zuri stayed silent. In this new country, she had already learned that a bowed head was safer than a raised voice.

When Zuri's hours at the janitorial job were cut, her paycheck shrank to almost nothing. What little she earned went straight to rent, nearly 70 percent of her income, leaving almost nothing for food, transportation, or school supplies. Every month was a race against the due date. When she finally fell behind, the landlord started leaving her messages. She had seen other tenants work off their rent by doing repairs around the building, but when she offered to do the same, he waved her off. "That's men's work," he said. A week later, an eviction notice appeared on her door.

The next apartment was worse: one bedroom in a neighborhood thick with sirens. She tried to make it a home anyway, pinning up drawings her children made at school, but that illusion shattered the night men broke in with guns drawn. Shaken, she gathered what little they owned and fled to a shelter an hour away, uprooting her children once again.

To keep them afloat, Zuri took a second job as a waitress, earning $2.33 an hour before taxes. Some nights, her tips barely covered the bus ride home. She didn't know that her employer was legally required to pay the difference when tips fell short of minimum wage. No one had told her, her employer didn't offer, and she didn't dare ask.

Like so many refugees, Zuri was expected to become self-sufficient almost immediately, despite the overwhelming challenges of resettlement. The U.S. refugee system is built on the principle of rapid employment, not long-term stability. Federal resources are designed to last roughly six months—covering basic needs like housing, food, and case management—but once that window closes, the support disappears. Resettlement agencies, under pressure to show quick results, urged refugees like Zuri to take whatever work they could find, usually low- or minimum-wage jobs that offered a fast paycheck. On paper, it looked like success: A job meant self-sufficiency. But in reality, it was existence. Five years on, many refugees end up worse off than when they first arrived, stuck in stagnant jobs.[12]

For women like Nwe Nwe and Zuri, priorities are grounded in survival, not in abstract notions of equality. Equal pay for equal work, the rallying cry in many labor movements, can feel distant or irrelevant when the urgent questions are: How do I safely earn a reliable living wage? How do I ensure my children can attend school? How do I keep my family from slipping into precarity? Their focus is on job quality, access to income, and protection from harm.

And yet, their struggles are not unique. Host-country women working the same low-wage jobs in crime-laden neighborhoods face the same undervaluation of labor, the same exposure to harassment, the same economic insecurity. The structural conditions that oppress refugee women also shape the lives of local women, creating overlapping experiences of exploitation.

But despite these shared hardships, solidarity rarely forms. The barriers are the very hierarchies that keep populations segregated. Refugee women rarely meet host-country women in a context that allows collective action; local women rarely see displaced neighbors as partners in a shared struggle. As a result, parallel hierarchies of disadvantage persist, where women experience the same oppression but never recognize a common cause.

Solidarity is fractured. Social psychologists studying in-group bias have long observed that people tend to stick to their own. My grandmother never visited Lakshmi's home, Thai garment workers never met Nwe Nwe's children, and the caseworker who initially helped Zuri never spoke to her again.

Beyond the lines we draw around ourselves, there's another wall holding women and girls back: the one inside. It's the quiet voice that says, *You don't belong*, the learned belief in second-class status. That voice doesn't come from nowhere. It's built from years of being told, explicitly and implicitly, that our worth depends on our skin color, our background, our gender. These messages start early and stick deep. They shape how we see ourselves. They reinforce the barriers already out there. Culture, media, and social norms don't just teach us our *place* within the social strata; they teach us not to question them. And the damage runs deeper than confidence. It strikes at agency itself: the belief that we can fight back, speak up, or even imagine something different.

I remember when I was sixteen, working after school and

on weekends at Walgreens. The drugstore, just a five-minute drive from my home, closed at 10 p.m. I was saving money for college and helping support my eldest sister while she was in medical school. One Wednesday night, I locked up and headed home. Just as I turned my mom's Honda Accord onto our street, a police car siren erupted behind me. Startled, I pulled over right in front of my house. The officer, a tower of a man, demanded that I open the car door. As I moved to comply, he yanked me out and pinned me against the car, his elbow digging into my back.

I was dressed in my Walgreens uniform, a stiff-collared dark blue polo emblazoned with the company logo and standard khaki pants. He questioned my recent whereabouts. Terrified, I replied that I had just come from work around the corner. Our neighbor Ximena, a Mexican immigrant, looked out her window, saw what was happening, and approached out of concern. She called out, "Can I help, officer? I know this girl." In response, the officer drew his gun, aimed it at her face, and ordered her back into her house. She complied. His power was limitless, and Ximena and I both knew that there would be consequences for asking questions.

Finding nothing more to pursue, the cop left after issuing me a citation: I had forgotten to turn on my headlights. I ran inside, shaking. The officer had used his position because he could. He was a Black man, and I was young, brown, and a girl. None of the interaction was about enforcing traffic laws. It was a masculine display of dominance. Afterward, neither Ximena nor I filed a complaint. We feared repercussions and held no illusions regarding fairness. We understood our place, and the invisible walls inside us thickened.

Years passed. My two older sisters became doctors, I graduated from college, and one April afternoon, I found myself enjoying apple tea at a café in Istanbul's posh Sultanahmet district. I was there visiting my twin sister, who was wrapping up her study abroad semester at Boğaziçi University. We were at a table with a couple of friends, all of us in our early twenties. My sister and I, along with an English friend, were dressed in baggy, shapeless outfits that reached our ankles and past our wrists, topped off with hijabs. In contrast, our Turkish friend wore a pair of tight black jeans with a fitted black tank top set against her pale skin and long, midnight-black hair.

Three sharply dressed Turkish men, probably in their thirties, were seated nearby. It wasn't long, minutes, before one of them got up, came over, and in English offered, "My friends and I would like to invite you to our table." Our Turkish friend replied in Turkish, then politely added in English, "No, thank you."

The atmosphere shifted. The man's friends closed in, looming over us, their presence pressing in.

"Decent women don't frequent cafés like this," one remarked.

Another chimed in, "If you aren't looking for male company, you shouldn't draw attention to yourselves."

"You should go to a proper Turkish restaurant," another suggested, referring to restaurants that featured separate sections for women and families. A jolt of fear shot through me. My heart raced, my stomach knotted. But the fear quickly turned to anger.

My sister had tried to prepare me for this moment. When I first landed in Istanbul and entered her cozy dorm room, which was decked with a plush, deep red Turkish rug and matching floor pillows, she handed me a pair of wide-legged pants that hung loosely from the waist, a shapeless loose-sleeved shirt that draped over the shoulders, and a headscarf. I received strict instructions: "Never smile at men; they see it as an invitation. Avoid eye contact; it insults their authority. Look down whenever you can. When asked, say you are from Pakistan." As Pakistanis, we would be seen as Muslims from a neighboring country, while Americans were often stereotyped as having loose morals and being overly sexualized. There was noticeable anxiety in my sister's voice. It all seemed too odd; between us, she was the outgoing, adventurous, and defiant one. What had changed during her six months in Istanbul?

Eventually, the men returned to their table, but only after a few more insults. Our Turkish friend said nothing, but she held the men's gaze until they parted, her eyes signaling a deafening *You don't own me*.

Each of us responded differently. My sister seemed resigned; she had clearly experienced this a hundred times before. Our English friend wanted to leave, to avoid more unwanted attention; she had reached her limit of toying with the status quo. And I wanted to throw water in their faces, but given my sister's earlier lecture, I thought better of it. As for our Turkish friend, she chose resistance: She called the waiter over and ordered more dolma and ekmek for the table. We were staying.

In that café, we had crossed the unseen line that dictated what physical spaces women could occupy and how we should behave. My sister had thought our conservative attire would shield us, render us unnoticed as a means of containment. It didn't work. Stepping out of the prescribed social order had invited backlash.

Refugee women confront similar psychological hurdles. And they cope with them using the same strategies we turned to in that café, or that Ximena and I relied on with the police officer—strategies that reflect how little or how much power we think we have: avoid, contain, accept, or resist.

In the end, the entrenchment of women's social subjugation, whether in Turkey, India, Brazil, or Thailand, is everywhere. We live with walls that divide us as women, and invisible walls within us that hold us back from claiming our own power. These walls, shaped by race, class, culture, and societal expectations, often make us doubt our right to occupy the same spaces, access the same opportunities, and claim the same resources as anyone else. But we do have that right.

I've come to believe that these "invisible walls," both real and internalized, keep women from connecting with those who could be allies and accomplices in the aspiration for equity. They limit our capacity to act collectively, leaving power scattered and untapped. Yet, when we consciously break through these barriers, we start to see that solidarity is a strategy, a way to challenge the inequities that keep some women at the margins.

This is why collective resistance matters. It requires moving beyond avoidance, quiet endurance, or acceptance, and toward joint action. Reimagining our shared identity as women, seeing beyond the divisions imposed upon us, and recognizing our common struggles and strengths.

For refugee women, for women at the bottom of social hierarchies, and for all women everywhere, this is how we start to level the playing field: by claiming our power individually, supporting each other boldly, and resisting collectively.

PART 2

What It Takes to Level the Playing Field

5

Change the Rules of the Game

The dirt streets of Kampala stretch endlessly, framed by the cracked window in the back seat of the worn-down Toyota. The air is thick with dust kicked up by passing motorbikes and handcarts heavy with goods. The dust clings to my skin, mixing with a heat that presses down like a heavy blanket; every breath feels labored. My colleagues ride quietly with me, the hum of the engine and the rhythmic jostling of the car the only sounds as we drive away from a bustling community center for refugees, a modest but vital space serving as school, clinic, and legal aid office.

As we turn a corner, my eyes are drawn to a figure walking along the side of the road. A woman, tall and painfully thin, her body almost skeletal. She wears a traditional Somali sari, the fabric faded, its once-vibrant hues now muted by sunlight. A scarf rests loosely over her head, slipping slightly as she cradles a child in her arms. The child's tiny head lolls weakly against the woman's chest, its small frame fragile. Behind the woman is another child, clutching the frayed edge of his mother's sari. His bare feet kick up dust as he follows her in dutiful silence, his gaze fixed on the ground.

My eyes drift to the woman's feet. She wears rubber flip-flops, the flimsy kind sold in crowded street markets, the soles nearly translucent, thin as paper. I find myself wondering how far she has walked in search of help. How many miles in this unforgiving heat, carrying her children?

The car jolts over a pothole, drawing me back. I blink back hot tears as a sharp anger slices through me: I hate poverty. I hate how it strips people of their dignity, leaving them to fight for survival with nothing but their resolve. I hate how women are forced to bear the brunt of it, women who carry the weight not just of their children, but of an entire life that offers them nothing but obstacles: worn-out shoes, frail bodies, and whatever strength they can summon to take one more step.

Displacement may always be part of our world, but the way we respond to it doesn't have to stay the same. The challenge can feel vast, but so is our capacity for change.

Reforming systems may not sound revolutionary but it is. Real change begins with transforming the very laws, policies, and institutions that shape our economies and societies, reorienting them to center women.

For displaced women, this means the right to work, to own property, to sell informally, to open a bank account, and to move freely without fear of detention or exploitation. These are basic building blocks of stability. When women have legal status and protection under the law, they can earn a living, send their children to school, and plan for the future. I saw this truth come to life in the summer of 2011 in Johannesburg, where I met Ayaan. I was studying how refugee women build resilience, and she was leading clandestine gatherings for Somali women. The meetings rotated from one home to another, always before the men returned from work. Somali women were expected to remain invisible in public: quiet, compliant, deferential. But who were they when those norms were lifted, even briefly? To find out, I meet them in private, in the spaces where they could speak freely.

At my first meeting, the room pulsed with energy. The women's voices rose in laughter, their smiles wide and unrestrained, a stark contrast from their public persona.

Ayaan stood out. She wore a flowing, rust-colored abaya, her black headscarf loosely framing her face. "This is my house," she began proudly, glancing around at the women seated on a thin, floral rug that had seen better days. "My family in the USA sends me money to support my business. I buy goods from Chinese traders and sell them in the Somali market." She paused, locking eyes with each woman. "My husband divorced me because I earn money. Because I am strong. The elders said he should get everything, the house, the business, and I should leave. But I hired a South African lawyer. I kept my things."

Ayaan lived in a close-knit, conservative Somali enclave in Johannesburg, a community held together by Xeer, the ancient code of customary law. Customary law is the unwritten rules and traditions that people in a community have followed for centuries to settle disputes and maintain peace among clans and families. When conflicts happened, whether it was about land, marriage, or physical violence, people brought their issues to elders. Ayaan had seen it all before: wives sent back to abusive husbands, daughters denied inheritance, survivors silenced for the sake of family honor.

A few decades ago, women in South Africa, particularly Black women, lived under a system of entrenched inequality and legalized discrimination. Prior to the 1996 Constitution, women were effectively treated as second-class citizens. Under both common and customary law, married women were classified as legal minors, requiring the consent of their husbands or male relatives to own property, sign contracts, or make decisions about their children.

For Black women, apartheid was not just a political system; it was something that reached into the home. Many families were split apart by the migrant labor system, which required men to travel far from where they lived in order to find work. Husbands disappeared into distant mines or cities for months at a time. Wives and children stayed behind. Most Black women labored as domestic workers in white households or bent over crops in agricultural fields. The jobs were poorly paid and rarely came with contracts, benefits, or protection. If a woman became pregnant, she could be dismissed without warning.

And yet, over the past quarter century, the country has changed for women in ways that would have once seemed unimaginable. The adoption of the 1996 Constitution was followed by laws that extended maternity leave, strengthened protections against domestic violence and sexual harassment, and established equal property rights. Today, women can sign contracts, start businesses, and manage their own finances without seeking male permission.

These reforms have reshaped the social landscape. According to international measures that track women's legal rights, such as the World Bank's Women, Business, and the Law index, South Africa now scores far higher than in the past, moving from 38 to 88 out of 100, placing it among the top ten global reformers in advancing gender equality.

But laws on paper do not automatically rewrite custom. For Ayaan, claiming those new freedoms required something more personal. She would have to challenge the invisible walls that had long defined her place. Legal rights gave her permission. What she needed next was the courage to use them. She would need to be defiant.

For me, defiance is a muscle. A muscle that strengthens each time a woman refuses to accept fewer rights because of a circumstance at birth—her gender, her race, her class, her passport.

For me, defiance has never been about shouting the loudest. It's quieter than that, more deliberate. It's the moment you feel that knot in your stomach and decide to speak anyway. It's the choice to question a rule that was never written with you in mind. It's saying *no*—not out of rebellion, but out of recognition that compliance has never kept us safe.

Still, I know that defiance isn't equally available to everyone. Some women can afford to risk disapproval, even punishment. Others risk everything, jobs, safety, even their lives. Privilege softens the fall, while poverty and displacement make the landing brutal. That's why those invisible walls between us of race, class, and status must come down. Until they do, the most vulnerable women will continue to shoulder the heaviest cost for resistance.

But even knowing the risks, I believe defiance is something children of all genders must be taught. From an early age, defiance is how children explore boundaries, test authority, and begin to form a sense of self. When supported, that skill evolves into integrity, the courage to speak up, to question the rules, to challenge injustice even when doing so comes at a cost. It's the internal compass that guides us to act when something doesn't sit right, and it's the backbone that allows us to make hard, courageous decisions.

I learned that many times over. I was fourteen when a teacher asked about my parents. When I told her I didn't have a father, she looked at me with pity and said dismissively, "That's too bad. You'll never amount to anything." I still remember the heat that rose in my chest and up my face. I didn't have the words for it then, but something in me said *No.* No to her small idea of who gets to succeed.

Years later, on a train in Berlin, I heard that voice again. Two men were harassing a young woman while everyone else looked away. I was twenty myself. The train car was silent except for their laughter. And then the voice came back, firm and familiar: *No.* Not this time. Not on my watch. So, I stood up between them and her. When they moved, I moved, a physical barrier. I refused to let fear decide what was acceptable. That moment, like so many others, reminded me that defiance isn't about anger—it's about refusal. Refusal to let silence masquerade as safety. Refusal to live by rules that were never meant for our liberation.

Defiance is how we make rights real, not just written into law but lived in practice. And when we practice it together, when defiance becomes collective, that's when the ground beneath power begins to shift.

For Ayaan, standing up for herself came with risks, but not the same kind others in her community faced. She had a business of her own and family abroad, a safety net she could fall back on if things went wrong. Most Somali women didn't have that.

In many cultures, survival is built on connection, on family, faith, and clan. These networks are both shield and shackle. They can provide food, money, and a place to sleep, but they can also close ranks against anyone who dares to step outside tradition. To step outside the expectations in this Somali community was to risk being cut off from the very web that kept you alive. The price of disobedience was isolation. And isolation, for a refugee woman in a foreign city, could be lethal.

Still, at that meeting in Johannesburg, it was clear that the women gathered in that small apartment wanted what Ayaan had: choices. They wanted safety that didn't require silence, stability that didn't depend on submission.

Gossip had already spread through the community about Ayaan, how she had stood up to her husband, faced down the elders, kept her business. The women had come not just to talk but to learn.

They spoke of things that could not be spoken elsewhere: beatings, rape, husbands with other wives, HIV, the quiet hunger of being trapped. One woman whispered that she wanted to open a bank account in her own name; could she do that without her husband finding out? Another asked what would happen if she left him altogether.

Ayaan didn't tell them what to do. She simply shared what she had learned. "The law is the way out," she said. "It's not perfect, but it protects me more than our community does. That's why I still have my house. My shop."

I remember how the room went quiet then, the way faces softened into something like disbelief. Some had never heard that the law could be theirs too, that the rights fought for by South African women extended to them, as legal residents.

Week by week, that secret gathering turned into something more, a self-help group. The women began sharing what they knew about their rights, trading advice, teaching each other to read and to budget. Watching them, I realized that thriving isn't just about access to education or work, though those things matter. It's about having choices, the power to decide for yourself what kind of life to live. They needed laws, policies, institutions that would open the doors they were already brave enough to knock on.

In 2011, my research led me to Hamid, a wealthy Somali businessman in Johannesburg. Tall and lean, in his mid-forties, authority rested easily on his shoulders. He owned several businesses, and his position in the Somali community was unquestioned.

It was midday when I arrived at his home. The living room was bright, the air filled with the scent of cardamom and incense, and Quranic verses in gold letters were neatly framed on the walls. His wife, a soft-spoken woman, never shared her name, but ushered me silently in, offered tea, and then vanished as I sat cross-legged in the stillness.

When Hamid entered, the atmosphere changed, his self-assured confidence filling the room. He invited me to stay for lunch, then called for his wife, his voice firm. When she forgot to bring a soft drink, a luxury that signified social status, he snapped at her sharply. She moved silently, setting each dish before us, never sitting to eat.

As we talked, I asked about the economic lives of Somali refugees, about the challenges women and men faced in earning a living or accessing loans. Hamid spoke with ease, his answers smooth. Each word carried an undertone of ownership that his wealth and status granted him, over people, lives, or knowledge.

When I asked if I could speak with his wife, he didn't answer me, just spoke her name, one word. I said "his wife" reluctantly, knowing she was far more than that. She appeared right away, as if she'd been standing just beyond the room, waiting. I asked what a typical day looked like for her. Hamid answered for her, describing her duties, her gratitude, her peace. She nodded along. Sometimes power can make silence seem like harmony.

Hamid reminded me so much of my uncles. While I was growing up with just my mom and sisters, our world felt softer, more collaborative. So, when we visited family in India, I was always struck by how my uncles carried themselves, as if every question in the room were meant for them, with everyone waiting to hear what *they* thought. My uncles never needed to raise their voices. Their authority was assumed. They filled a room the way Hamid did, not through cruelty, but through certainty.

That memory came rushing back, as I watched the stark contrast between Ayaan and Hamid. Hamid's power was inherited through his gender, wealth, and tribal status. He shared it only so long as it reinforced the very norms that kept him on top. His authority depended on the silence of others.

Ayaan's power was earned by claiming legal rights and bending them toward her own survival. The rights she relied on, property ownership, the ability to open a business, to keep her earnings, had been hard-won by South African women long before her arrival. Those women had fought to make the system fairer, and in doing so, they had paved the way for Ayaan too.

Hamid used power to preserve order, Ayaan to disrupt it. Hamid guarded his position; Ayaan multiplied hers. Where his influence depended on keeping women compliant, hers grew by helping women question compliance itself. The difference was everything. That was the difference between inherited power and claimed power. One protects itself by keeping others small; the other expands by teaching others to stand taller. We each hold some form of claimed power.

Legal rights offer women safer choices. Without those rights, every decision becomes a gamble. I've seen this pattern repeat across countries and contexts. Grace, in Nairobi, sold used clothes on the street because she wasn't legally allowed to work. Each day she faced harassment from police and predatory customers. In Irbid, ten-year-old Yassi worked twelve-hour shifts in a bakery because, as a child, she was least likely to be detained. And in Mae Sot, Nwe Nwe labored in a garment factory for a fraction of a living wage because it was the only alternative to hunger in the camp. None of these women lacked strength or defiance. What they lacked were legal rights, the kind that protect, empower, and make room for safer, more dignified choices.

Our goal should never be to decide what women *ought* to do with their lives. The point is to give them the knowledge and options so that *they* can decide what works best for them.

So, what happens when women are afforded legal rights from the start? Would they be safer? Would they be able to earn to their potential, to choose, plan, and rebuild on their own terms? Around the world, there are places trying to answer those very questions.

On February 24, 2022, Vladimir Putin invaded Ukraine. It was the largest attack on European soil since World War II, a simultaneous ground and air assault on a civilian population. In just ten days, one million Ukrainians fled to neighboring Poland, and within two years, more than four million would be displaced across Europe.

By the time I landed in Warsaw in May 2022, the signs of this mass exodus were everywhere. Every corner of the city carried traces of families uprooted, lives suddenly on hold. I knew from experience that the initial wave of aid—focused on food, shelter, and immediate relief—wouldn't last. Despite the early optimism that the war might end in a matter of months, I knew it would drag on much longer. After all, the average length of displacement is twenty years, the time it typically takes before it's safe enough for people to return home.

In the coming months, humanitarian efforts would be stretched thin. The initial outpouring of aid would eventually dry up or be overwhelmed by the volume of people in need. It became clear to me that the newcomers would soon have to find work to sustain themselves. With nine out of ten displaced Ukrainians being women and children, given most men stayed behind to fight or support the war effort, these women would face significant risks, especially without legal protections.

Then something happened that surprised most, including me: Europe united. Ukrainians were welcomed with open arms. This was distinctly unlike what had happened when Syrian refugees had sought safety in Europe a few years prior. Back then, only Germany truly stepped up to welcome them, while other countries tried to push them out or move them along as quickly as possible, often with brute force. This time, Europe responded differently. Borders were opened, accommodation was made, and most crucially, legal rights were extended.

Within two weeks of the invasion, the Council of the European Union granted legal status to displaced Ukrainians in all EU countries. This decision was historic. It meant the Ukrainians had unfettered access to jobs, social services, and essential public benefits. They could work, travel, and live freely within the European Union, bypassing the often agonizingly slow asylum process.

Poland, hosting the largest Ukrainian population, did not just accept its Ukrainian neighbors; it embraced them. Ukrainian flags flew beside Polish ones on government buildings. Polish volunteers in bright vests flooded train stations, bus depots, and malls, ready to answer questions and offer assistance. Tens of thousands of Polish homeowners joined a government program to house Ukrainians, receiving a modest subsidy—40 zloty (8 U.S. dollars) per boarder per day.[1] The government provided refugees with a one-time 300-zloty (77 U.S. dollars)[2] cash boost, free train travel, and fast-tracked national ID numbers, which were essential for landing jobs and accessing services like healthcare and education. Companies launched internship programs for refugees and formed special recruitment teams to connect newcomers with jobs.

Everywhere I went, I saw small acts of generosity. Local shopkeepers posted signs in their windows like the one outside a grocer's pop-up food bank: "Please take an item from your bag to help feed our Ukrainian guests." Almost every Pole I met was contributing—donating money, making supply runs to the border, offering hot meals, or collecting coats and blankets for the displaced. According to one study, more than two-thirds of Poles helped in some way.[3]

I met Anastasia in Warsaw. The city was overflowing, and housing was stretched thin. Anastasia bounced between hotel rooms, never staying more than a couple of nights. Mornings were spent at her temporary remote job; evenings were for job hunting. Even the simplest tasks, like getting a SIM card, securing reliable internet, and finding a quiet spot for interviews, became mentally exhausting hurdles.

In May, her persistence paid off. She landed a job at a Fortune 100 company, putting her master's degree in international management to use. Like six out of ten Ukrainian women, Anastasia had completed university.[4] But education alone wasn't enough. It was the right to work that turned survival into a thriving career.

Not all displaced Ukrainians were ready to return to careers right away; they lived in a haze, with concentration and focus out of reach. The war was too close, too overwhelming. PTSD and acute panic attacks were common. The women still heard the sirens and anguished over loved ones left behind—a father, brother, husband, or son—fighting and unreachable. Anxiety kept most glued to social media. They lived in an in-between space, physically present, emotionally detached.

Committing to a professional job felt too permanent, too much like a betrayal of hope. They might return to Ukraine, maybe on Friday? Most opted for temporary work. Women took jobs as cleaners, kitchen workers, servers, and farmhands. This meant lower wages, yes, but also, at the same time, self-determination. They could choose the type of work that suited their situation. Two years into the war, many were ready to rebuild their careers, and thanks to the systems the government had put in place, it was an option open to them.

At the onset of the war the Blue Dot centers set up in Warsaw by UNHCR and UNICEF were a lifeline. Inside these spaces, Ukrainian women and children could meet with caseworkers who helped them with the essentials: meal vouchers, applications for a national ID, housing assistance, medical appointments, and cash support. There was childcare on-site, a relief for mothers trying to focus on piecing together a semblance of stability.

The difference the Blue Dot centers made was notable. Instead of navigating endless lines in unfamiliar offices, shuffling from one government agency to the next, these women could find everything they needed under one roof. The benefit wasn't just about saving time; it was about preserving the energy and mental and emotional strength they so desperately needed to keep going.

As of 2024, 680,000 Ukrainian children were enrolled in Poland's public schools, 69 percent of Ukrainian refugees had secured formal employment, and Poland had seen a decrease in unemployment alongside an increase in wages for its citizens.[5] These milestones highlight a fundamental truth: When refugees are supported with services and legal rights, they contribute, integrate, and thrive. Access to education and work isn't just about meeting basic needs; it's about strengthening communities.

In 2015, when Syrians fleeing civil war risked everything to reach Europe, only Germany, under Chancellor Angela Merkel, welcomed them. While other nations hesitated or pushed them out, Germany took in nearly one million

Syrians, offering not just shelter, but permanent residency, the right to work, and unemployment benefits.

Germany didn't stop at access to legal status and public services, though. It invested. Refugees were provided tailored mental health programs, German-language classes, and free vocational training to support their inclusion.

And it wasn't just the government. More than half the German population contributed; ordinary people did extraordinary things.[6] They flooded reception centers, offering help with job searches, organizing clothing drives, and repairing bicycles so newcomers could get around freely. They showed up to teach German, but also swimming, guitar, and everyday life skills, knowing that dignity is built through connection and confidence. Locals accompanied refugees to hospitals, helped them navigate unfamiliar systems, and created coffee hours in neighborhood churches, where Syrians could practice German in a welcoming space. They stood on train platforms with bags of clothes, medicine, and sandwiches, greeting families who had lost everything with a simple but profound message: *You are welcome here*. In Kassel, my husband's hometown, a group of volunteer psychologists and doctors formed the Centre for Psychosocial Support of Refugees.

Within seven years, 95 percent of displaced Syrian children were in school. Seventy-three percent of refugee men were employed (though only 29 percent of women), many moved up from low-wage work. Seventy-five percent of those employed worked in skilled positions, in high-demand sectors such as healthcare, logistics, and the social work.[7] The German Institute for Economic Research projected a 0.5 percent increase in gross domestic product (GDP) over the next decade, tied directly to refugee inclusion. On average, a refugee in Germany contributes €3,300 ($3,850) more per year than they receive in benefits.[8] Germany has shown that when refugees are given rights and the opportunity to work, they don't drain economies; they can strengthen them.

In 2018, Colombia launched its Temporary Protection Status for 1.7 million Venezuelans, granting them legal residency until 2031. Since the permits were enacted, Venezuelan incomes increased by 35 percent and formal employment rose by 10 percent.[9] These rights matter for all refugees, but they matter even more for women, who face unique economic and legal barriers when displaced.

Across Poland, Germany, and Colombia, the pattern is unmistakable. When women are granted legal rights at the outset, when they are allowed to work, to enroll their children in school, to access healthcare, to move freely, and to open bank accounts, their choices expand. Safety ceases to be a gamble. Work becomes a pathway, not a risk. Anastasia did not thrive because she was unusually resilient; she thrived because the law cleared a path beneath her feet. Venezuelan women in Colombia did not suddenly become more industrious; they became newly authorized to participate. Legal rights do not guarantee ease, but they convert desperation into decision-making. And when women can choose—where to work, how to care for their families, how to rebuild—the benefits ripple outward. Children enroll in school, businesses gain skilled workers, tax bases grow, neighborhoods stabilize, and host economies strengthen. The evidence is clear: When women begin with rights, they build not only their own futures but the prosperity of the communities that receive them. Without those rights, every step is perilous. With them, entire societies move forward.

6

The Power of Choice

Organizations working in crisis zones, whether in refugee camps, conflict areas, or disaster sites, operate under a set of internationally recognized guidelines called the Sphere Standards. Developed in the late 1990s, these standards define the *minimum standards* for survival: 15 liters of safe water per person per day, ensuring a maximum of twenty people per shared toilet facility, 3.5 square meters of covered living area per person, and so on.

These standards reveal how the humanitarian system defines well-being, primarily through the lens of survival. Similar to the Sphere Standards, the poverty reduction industry's obsession is with minimum income. In poverty work, economists use the poverty line, a fixed income threshold, to determine who counts as poor, ultra-poor, or non-poor.

And just as humanitarian agencies often struggle to move beyond emergency relief toward long-term development, the global poverty industry has struggled to move beyond the idea that a few extra dollars a day can fix structural inequality. Both systems, in their own way, have institutionalized minimum standards, and in doing so, risk mistaking sustenance for success. We know, especially in the case of women, that more income doesn't always mean individual agency. A woman may earn more and still face violence at home, harassment on her way to work, or lack access to childcare and healthcare. For women like Grace in Nairobi or Farah in Zarqa, income alone cannot buy choice.

It wasn't until recently that economists began to understand poverty as complex and multidimensional. In 2010, the United Nations adopted the concept of multidimensional poverty, measuring deprivation across health, education, living standards, and access to essential services. This approach recognized that poverty is interconnected, shaped by access to food, water, safety, housing, justice, and political representation.

Yet even with this broader lens, poverty can feel overwhelmingly too big, too systemic, too far beyond any individual's control. Within this paradigm, it's easy to lose sight of personal agency, because if poverty touches every aspect of life, how can any one person possibly climb out of it?

The second challenge is that most humanitarian and development organizations tend to focus on one issue, education, health, or livelihoods, without connecting it to the others. We train farmers to improve their harvests but ignore how they'll get their crops to market. We empower women to start microbusinesses but rarely bring men along on the journey toward gender equity.

The third challenge is in program design. Humanitarian efforts often focus exclusively on services for refugees, even when they live alongside ultra-poor host communities, unintentionally creating segregation instead of fostering inclusion. By isolating participants from peers of different backgrounds or income levels, we limit their exposure to new networks, skills, and opportunities. Refugees, after all, live in *communities*, not in silos.

We can hold both truths at once: that inequality is structural, and that women still have the power to shape their futures when they have access to real choices. Women like Ayaan and Farah already know what they need to thrive. Women like Ayaan and Farah do not need outsiders to sketch the blueprint of a good life on their behalf. They already understand what safety means for their children, what dignified work looks like, what kind of future they hope to build. What they often lack are the structural conditions that allow those aspirations to take shape.

The aim, then, is not prescription but empowerment, to remove the barriers that constrain their choices. That means ensuring legal recognition and enforceable rights. It means access to decent, stable work—not just any income, but employment that pays a living wage and offers basic protections. It means inclusion in decision-making spaces where policies about housing, labor, migration, and education are debated and decided. These are scaffolds. They expand the realm of the possible without dictating the outcome.

These foundations matter. How those elements are prioritized, sequenced, and pursued will differ from woman to woman. Ayaan may prioritize flexible work hours that allow her to care for family. Farah may focus first on credential recognition.

Imagine you're Maria, a former nurse from Colombia. You've fled everything you've known in order to protect your family. Now you stand in Nueva Loja, a dusty town near the border in northern Ecuador, facing an uncertain future. This place is gritty, with crime and sex work as pervasive as the humid air. The oil industry looms over everything, from the chaotic markets to the bustling bars, casting a long shadow over the town.

The heat bears down on you as you clutch the hands of your two children, both exhausted from the long, difficult journey. This place isn't home, but you hope it's where you can start over, far from the violence and fear that once ruled your life. In Nueva Loja, you're not alone: One in five residents is a Colombian refugee like you, many of whom fled decades ago, during the first wave of the 1980s exodus.

For decades, members of FARC terrorized your country. Their name (which translates to "the Revolutionary Armed Forces of Colombia—People's Army") was whispered with fear, the group tied to kidnappings, bombings, and brutal assassinations. They financed their war through engaging in the cocaine trade and extorting ordinary people like you. When the FARC paramilitaries came, they demanded money, and everyone knew what would happen if you couldn't pay. So, when they came for you, you ran.

Your husband abandoned his business, and you left your job. You moved from place to place, never settling, always looking over your shoulder, never sure how long your safety would last. The fear of being found, of having nowhere left to run, haunted you even in the rare moments of peace.

After months of uncertainty and danger, you finally crossed the border into Ecuador, hoping for a fresh start. Nueva Loja, though far from perfect, gave you a small sense of relief. Here, you could stop running. For the first time in what felt like forever, you began to think beyond mere survival. You started to consider reclaiming the life you had lost.

Now you face a new challenge: how to rebuild. This isn't just about choosing your own adventure; it's about creating a foundation for yourself and your family, one decision at a time. Unlike in the popular choose-your-own-adventure kids' books, where the options presented to readers result in benign redirection of the narrative, the stakes here are higher.

You hear from your neighbor, another Colombian woman who arrived years before, about a local group that supports Colombian families trying to find their footing. "Go speak to them," she says. "They helped me."

A few says later, you meet a caseworker, and she offers something that feels like a lifeline, a chance to join the Graduation Model, a program designed to help refugee families like yours rebuild their lives step by step. It begins with immediate relief—food vouchers and financial support to cover rent and keep the lights on. The constant edge of panic begins to soften. From there, you attend workshops to build practical skills. You receive a small business grant and are connected to a savings account in your own name. A coach meets with you regularly, helping you set realistic goals, troubleshoot setbacks, and plan for steady income.

With the daily scramble for food and rent eased, something shifts. For the first time, you can begin to imagine not just getting through the week but building a future.

The program offers two paths: You can either join a vocational skills program to find a job, or you can work in a cooperative with other women.

Do you:

1. Choose the vocational skills program? (Go to Choice 1.)

2. Join a cooperative of women? (Go to Choice 6.)

CHOICE 1: BUILD YOUR SKILLS

You decide it's time to take control of your future. The vocational skills program feels like a way to rebuild and create stability for you and your family. After talking with your coach, you enroll in a course focused on Microsoft Office and customer relationship management software. There's high demand for these skills in call centers, and while it's not the nursing career you left behind, it feels like the right fit. You know that working in a call center can offer a livable wage, enough to cover rent, food, healthcare, and transportation. Most important, the job would allow you to work from home, safely away from the streets of Nueva Loja. It's a chance to use the communication and customer service skills you've always had.

The course is challenging but promising. As you practice navigating spreadsheets and databases, a sense of hope stirs within you.

But you're able to work only part-time, as your afternoons are dedicated to caring for the girls, aged eight and ten, once they return from school. Fortunately, your husband has found work as a day laborer on a construction site, and together, you two earn enough to get by.

The Graduation Model program also offers you an

additional course to help you launch a small business, providing a grant to get you started.

Do you decide to take on this extra course and set up your own business?

1. Decline the offer and focus on building stability with your current job. (Go to Choice 2.)

2. Accept the challenge and start a small business alongside your call center work. (Go to Choice 3.)

CHOICE 2: DECLINE THE EXTRA COURSE

Your coach advises that having more than one income source is important, but you feel relieved to finally have some stability, and you decline the offer. A few months later, however, your husband is injured on the job. You borrow money from neighbors to cover medical costs, and while you have three months of cash support remaining from the Graduation Model program, his recovery will take six.

As the cash support ends and your savings run out, you're unable to pay rent. Forced to move, you begin selling cigarettes outside bars in the evenings, bringing your daughters along to help. The work is degrading, and both you and the girls are regularly harassed. Men force the girls to sit in their laps, and you are often assumed to be a prostitute because of your Colombian background. You feel trapped, wishing there were another way to make enough money, but your family's needs are urgent. You make the decision to take a step back and begin again.

Dead end: Return to Choice 1.

CHOICE 3: ACCEPT THE CHALLENGE AND START A BUSINESS

You decide to take on the extra course, recognizing the value of an additional income stream. The program teaches you how to budget and manage your finances, and it provides a small grant to help you launch a business. Remembering your days as a nurse, you come up with an idea: to design unique medical scrubs adorned with animals or popular characters.

With five hundred dollars in seed capital from the program, you bring your business plan to life, purchasing a sewing machine, fabric, and supplies. The business is launched slowly, but you gradually gain loyal customers. Things seem to be improving.

You begin to set aside money for large expenses like rent and emergencies; your coach calls it your "safety net." You understand how essential it is to have savings, just in case. But as your business grows, things at home take a turn. Your husband, once supportive, grows frustrated. He sees the steady income you're bringing in and begins demanding control over your money. His temper flares more often, and the tension in the household is thick. You fear for your and the girls' safety, unsure of what he might do next.

Do you:

1. Stand up to him and refuse to hand over your money? (Go to Choice 4.)

2. Give in to his demands to avoid conflict? (Go to Choice 5.)

CHOICE 4: REFUSE TO HAND OVER YOUR MONEY

You stand your ground and refuse to give in to your husband's demands. His anger flares, and this time, it turns violent. He beats you, and fear rushes through your body—but somehow, you find the strength to act. You know you can't stay any longer; the ongoing abuse has to stop. Shaken but determined, you grab the children and take them to a neighbor's house for safety. In desperation, you reach out to your coach, someone you've come to trust through the Graduation Model program.

Your coach listens with empathy and refers you to a local shelter that provides emergency housing for survivors of domestic violence. Unfortunately, the shelter is overcrowded, and there's space for you and your children for only three days. But in those few days, you start to figure out your next steps.

When your time at the shelter ends, your local church steps in, offering temporary housing while you search for a permanent place to live. They give you the space to regroup. But there's another challenge weighing heavily on you: your business. All your equipment and supplies are still with your husband, and he knows where you sell your scrubs. The fear of what he might do keeps you from going back to the market stall, leaving you feeling stuck and unsure of how to move forward.

Throughout this difficult journey, your coach becomes a trusted advisor and friend, helping you navigate both the emotional and practical challenges ahead. They help you break down into manageable steps the overwhelming task of restarting your business, and they encourage you to stay motivated through the setbacks.

They also support you through the challenges of enrolling your children in school, finding a new place to live, and ensuring you have the legal protections needed to stay safe. Each step feels like progress, helping you reclaim the independence that was taken from you.

In time, you find a new space to sell and slowly begin to rebuild. Customers who once loved your custom designs return. Your business begins to thrive once again. With the financial literacy skills you've learned, you manage your money wisely, save for the future.

And you've done it: You've graduated from the Graduation Model program! You are earning a stable income of eighty-six U.S. dollars per month, have a savings buffer of 5 percent, are eating three meals a day, and your daughters are enrolled in school. All this within eighteen months. Congratulations!

THE END.

CHOICE 5: AVOID CONFLICT

Unable to bear the constant tension, you give in to your husband's demands. He takes control of the money you've earned, and the resentment festers into violence. The abuse becomes more frequent, and soon your business begins to fall apart. The bright future you had envisioned fades as you feel trapped in a cycle of fear and helplessness.

You know you need help, but shame keeps you silent. Then one afternoon, your neighbor, who's also in the Graduation Model program, knocks on your door. She's noticed you've been keeping to yourself and just wants to check in.

At first, you brush her off, but her kindness lingers. The next time she stops by something in you softens. The story spills out, the fights with your husband, the bruises, the business slipping away. She doesn't flinch. She listens. Over several visits, she urges you gently but firmly to stop giving in to his demands, to reclaim your life.

Dead end: Go to Choice 4.

CHOICE 6: JOIN THE COOPERATIVE

Knowing that vocational training will take time, you join the local women's cooperative instead, hoping that working with others will provide you the support and guidance you desperately need. You've never run a business before, and the weight of responsibility and risk is overwhelming. At first, you feel like an outsider: The women are mostly Ecuadorians, and you're Colombian. But rather than keeping their distance, they welcome you warmly. Those with business savvy take you under their wing, patiently teaching you the ropes.

Together, you all decide to launch a business producing plantain chips, using a $3,500 grant from the program to kick-start the venture.

Your coach connects the cooperative with a local university, where you and the other women learn to access the market, design graphic labels, and operate modern machines that streamline production. Your coach even helps you apply for government support, securing three years of rent-free workspace, an invaluable boost for the business.

After six months of hard work, the production facility is

complete, with health code certifications proudly displayed. Each woman plays a specific role in the production line, and together you share responsibilities, make decisions, and celebrate your small victories as a team. Through this collaboration, you aren't just improving your standing in the marketplace; you're helping each other grow. Women with strong business skills mentor those more adept at production or labor, creating a supportive network where everyone has a vital role to play.

It takes a year before you begin to see any real income. Despite the steady growth, it isn't yet enough. Even with your husband's work as a day laborer, you still need extra income to make ends meet. Reluctantly, you pull your daughters from school so they can help sell plantain chips on the side of the road and at the bus terminal. It's a difficult choice, but you hope it's temporary.

Over time, your husband's frustration grows as your commitments to the cooperative keep you out of the home for long hours. His temper flares more frequently, and the tension in the household becomes unbearable. You fear for your safety, unsure of what he might do next.

Do you:

1. Stand up to him? (Go to Choice 7.)

2. Avoid conflict? (Go to Choice 5.)

CHOICE 7: STAND UP FOR YOURSELF

One day, you confide in the women of the cooperative about your husband's abuse. To your surprise, they don't hesitate.

They rally around you once again—this time, not just as business partners, but as friends concerned for your safety. They help you find the resources needed to leave the abusive situation and set up a safe place for you and your children. Their unwavering support gives you the strength you need to make a fresh start.

You reach out to your coach as well, someone you've come to trust deeply through the Graduation Model program. Your coach provides trauma-informed care, helping you navigate the challenges of enrolling your daughters in a new school and ensuring you have the legal protection needed to keep you safe. Each step forward feels like progress, helping you reclaim the independence that was taken from you.

Eighteen months have passed since you joined the Graduation Model program. You have achieved what once seemed impossible. The plantain chip business is now thriving. You're earning a stable income of eighty-six dollars per month, have a savings buffer of 5 percent, and are eating three meals a day. Most important, your daughters are back in school, safe and hopeful for their future.

THE END

Maria is a composite of a number of real women, and the Graduation Model is a real framework.

From the moment Maria arrived in Nueva Loja, her path was anything but straightforward. She faced poverty, instability, and fear, yet the support she received through the Graduation Model gave her choices that allowed her to transform her life.

What stands out for me about the Graduation Model is its recognition that meaningful transformation is built on stability. It understands that survival needs must be met first, so participants aren't consumed by hunger or housing insecurity. For Maria, securing her basic needs (food, shelter, and safety) gave her the mental space to invest in skills building, something unimaginable when you live day-to-day.

The program invests in women, offering not only skills training but also seed funding for those who want to start businesses. Having the option to learn marketable skills alongside financial literacy and business development opened possibilities for Maria, helping her increase her income potential and move closer to self-reliance.

For those who aren't entrepreneurial, the model provides the option for participants to work in groups, where collaboration can offset individual weaknesses. Its focus on financial management and savings gave Maria both control and a vital safety net, ensuring she could weather setbacks. This support gave her the tools to take control of her life, make informed decisions, and shape a future on her own terms.

At the same time, opening economic opportunities, while critical, didn't automatically ensure safety for Maria. New possibilities can also bring new risks. Through careful program monitoring, fostering social networks, and providing consistent support with safety planning, these risks can be minimized. For me, this reflects a deeper value: Dignity and opportunity should never come at the expense of personal safety. True empowerment must be rooted in protection.

7

Reshape Norms

When I was a kid, my mom would come home from her job, barely put her bag down before heading straight to the kitchen. While the rice steamed and lentils simmered, she'd be packing lunches for the next day, checking our homework, folding the laundry.

Some evenings women from the neighborhood would stop by. Some came to ask her for help setting up their first bank account. Others needed her to fill out a form or translate a letter. A few couldn't read or write, so my mother would have me or my sisters sit beside them and teach them how to sign their names. I must have been eight, maybe nine, tracing letters slowly with another woman's hand. It felt like a small thing, but looking back, I see it for what it was, a transfer of power, the kind that begins around the kitchen table.

Years later, working with women across the world, I saw the same pattern repeat itself in different forms. Whether in the crowded neighborhoods of Nairobi, the refugee camps of Jordan, or the mountain villages of Morocco, women tended to children, elders, husbands, and communities.

Women's work was *expected*. Society treated care as obligation, not contribution. Others felt entitled to their labor, as women's time and energy were part of the natural order of things. But these roles we think of as innate are not written in our DNA. They are shaped and reinforced by a collective agreement as social rules bestowed quietly from one generation to the next. They tell us what a "good woman" does, what a "good mother" sacrifices, and what a "respectable wife" endures. These roles we think of as natural are in fact constructed, reinforced, and passed down like inherited furniture. If they're made, they can be remade. I've seen it happen.

"The government doesn't build roads this far out," Abdelkhalk was saying. "The people here, when they need something, they build it." He pointed toward a terraced slope, where stone walls caught the morning sun. "That's their reservoir," he added. "They built it to store water for the entire community. It keeps their crops alive through the dry season." We were in Morocco, in 2007, driving at the edge of the High Atlas Mountains on a narrow, winding dirt road carved into the side of the mountain. A look down the cliff caught my heart in my throat. The drop was rugged, a blur of rock and shadow toward the valley below. I decided it was safer not to look. Instead, I fixed my eyes straight ahead, one hand gripping the interior door handle as the white Jeep Wrangler bounced along the hand-built road.

Abdelkhalk and I had arrived in the small village of Timicha Toundoute having set out from the city of Ouarzazate. As the crow flies, the distance we traveled was only about thirty miles, but the trip took two hours of rough driving.

The road wound past villages of mud-brick houses the color of the earth, their flat roofs stacked with drying herbs and barley. Terraced fields clung to the mountainside at improbable angles, green against the rust-colored stone. Women carried babies in slings on their backs while balancing bundles of firewood on their heads. The sun was rising and with it the temperature, but the view, in the pink glow of morning, left you breathless.

Abdelkhalk led the Participation de la Communauté la Réforme de l'Enseignement Primaire dans le Maroc (Community Participation in Primary Education Reform in Morocco) project. He had spent his career working in rural Morocco, helping communities organize themselves—farmers, herders, women's cooperatives—to improve their livelihoods and adapt to a changing climate. Over the years, his focus had shifted from improving livelihoods to improving governance: how local people make decisions, manage their shared resources, and ensure that women and youth lead.

Timicha Toundoute was home to about thirty Berber families. I sat cross-legged on the floor of the tearoom in the home of Malika and Mohammad, where the village council would soon gather to hear about our project. The house hummed with the soft rhythm of morning, children's laughter spilling from the courtyard, the faint clink of dishes, the rustle of fabric as Malika moved gracefully about, preparing breakfast. Her husband and four sons had just returned from morning prayers at the mosque, stopping in for a meal and the meeting before heading to the fields.

I cradled a small glass of mint tea, its warm sweetness cutting through the cool morning air, and watched the day unfold. Mohammad and Hassan, the eldest son, spoke quietly, arguing over whether the river was too low to use the village's water-powered mill. Perhaps one of them should take the family's donkey and a sack of barley to the diesel-powered grain mill four villages away. Little Rashida, Malika and Mohammad's eldest granddaughter, peeked into the tearoom with wide, curious eyes before Malika gently ushered her out.

Farming in the High Atlas Mountains required both ingenuity and endurance. Water is scarce, and the men work together to construct and maintain the irrigation systems that sustain their livelihoods. It's an effort that synchronizes rock, mud, water, and muscle. But just as the men labor, so do the women. In fact, they work longer days, and girls start helping at a younger age than boys.

Malika left the tearoom to gather vegetables from the kitchen garden for the midmorning meal, and after that, there was the barley harvest. Once the barley was cut and dried, it was the women's task to carry it on their backs to the threshing area, where mules would trample through it, separating grain from chaff. Afterward, the women would winnow the grain, grind it into flour, knead the flour into loaves, and bake the loaves in wood-fired ovens that required a constant supply; the task of gathering that wood fell to the girls.

At seven years old, little Rashida had already joined the older village girls to collect bundles of firewood and carry them down from the forest. She knew how to milk cows, gather fodder for the animals, and with her small hands, keep pace with the rhythm of pounding clothes clean in the river. There was a quiet inevitability to it all, a rhythm that had shaped not just her, but her mother and grandmother before her. For Rashida, marriage and motherhood awaited;

for her parents, the day she found a husband would mark their success as parents. She was being carefully raised into her future role as caregiver, wife, and mother.

Watching her, I could see the invisible threads of culture at work. These were rules that felt fixed, unchangeable, passed down as unquestioned truths. They quietly guided daily life, shaping actions, expectations, and interactions, often without anyone even realizing it.

The day before my visit with Malika and Mohammad, I met Safra, a twenty-seven-year-old teacher at the local primary school in Malika's village. The heat in the faded Pepto-Bismol-pink concrete building was stifling, and the room sparse, dominated by a large black chalkboard stretching across the front wall.

Safra came from another Berber village, Amezri, and held the distinction of being the first from her community to attend secondary school. She described the town where the secondary school was located as modern and bustling, a place where women worked outside the home and lived beyond the traditional constraints that had shaped her upbringing. "The roles assigned to women in my village—wives, mothers—kept them from reaching their true potential as human beings," Safra explained. "It didn't feel normal anymore." Her words lingered with me, prompting a deeper curiosity about how her sense of "normal" had shifted so profoundly.

Worldwide, 119 million girls are kept out of school. While nearly half of countries had achieved gender parity in primary education, the gap widens sharply as girls grow older; by high school only a fourth of girls are in classrooms.[1] For girls displaced by conflict, the odds are even harsher. In conflict-affected regions, girls are more than twice as likely to be out of school compared to their peers in stable settings. In Lebanon's Beqaa Valley, Syrian refugee children as young as three work in the fields to support their families, slipping past checkpoints meant to confine them to refugee settlements. Dyana, one of these child laborers, harvested potatoes. Each morning, she followed the rows of crops. When she described her dream, her voice softened. "I imagine a school to be very beautiful," she told me, "with paintings of girls and boys on the walls."

Her words landed deep in my chest. I wanted to promise her something—a classroom, a desk, a future that matched her imagination—but I had no such power. I swallowed back the heat rising behind my eyes. Beneath it, the familiar anger surfaced: not at her family, not at her country, but at the grinding machinery of poverty that narrows a child's world to a field of potatoes when it should stretch to painted walls and open books.

In Morocco in 2007, 65 percent of rural girls had never set foot in a classroom.[2] When Safra began teaching, only one girl attended the school. Determined to change this, Safra tirelessly visited each household, knocking on doors and speaking directly with parents. Despite her efforts, the impact was minimal. Why? Because norms are the rules of behavior that a group agrees upon, where shared expectations and reciprocal actions are reinforced. They are not held by one individual.

Safra did not give up. She found allies in my colleagues Hafida and Abdelkhalk. Hafida was the operations behind the project; nothing moved without her. Like Abdelkhalk, she was a Berber from the High Atlas Mountains. She understood the language, culture, and livelihoods of the villagers. Together, the trio began their efforts by engaging the gatekeepers of community tradition. They met with village councils (comprised of the eldest male from each family), the faqih (the religious leader), village associations, and school administrators.

The meeting at Malika and Mohammad's home began the way these conversations always did, with a practical appeal. Safra, our local education lead, spoke about the benefits of literacy. Most adults in the village couldn't read or write, so the examples she gave, reading a letter from a son working in Casablanca, calculating the right price for a sack of barley, or knowing which bus to take to the next town landed squarely.

Then an elderly man spoke up. "In a nearby village," he recalled, "while the men were away for the week working in Casablanca, a merchant came and bought the women's silver jewelry for almost nothing. They didn't know its true value." A ripple went through the crowd. Heads nodded. Slowly, the discussion widened. One elder pointed out that children were needed during harvest season. Another mentioned the lack of separate lavatories for girls and boys. A woman at the back added, shyly, "Our daughters collect firewood in the afternoons. How can they also go to school?" The list grew. Safra listened carefully, then explained how the project aimed to address these very challenges, lightening girls' workloads, improving school conditions, and finding ways to make education fit village life rather than disrupt it. The tone shifted; the idea began to feel more possible.

Over the following months, the real work began. Hafida, Abdelkhalk, and local leaders visited families across the mountains. Hafida drove the white Jeep along narrow, hand-chiseled roads, her hands steady on the wheel as cliffs dropped away just meters from the tires. Her presence as a woman behind the wheel, hair tucked under a scarf, eyes fixed on the horizon, was itself a quiet revolution. In each village, she and the local female teachers gathered families in town halls and courtyards. Abdelkhalk and the other male colleagues made a point of stepping aside, letting the women lead. These were small acts, but in a place where gender roles were rigidly drawn, they felt momentous, tiny fissures in an old, unyielding order.

When Hafida introduced the idea of creating parent-teacher associations (PTA), the elders hesitated. And to be fair, so did the women. Women on a committee? That was new territory for everyone. The room went quiet for a moment. The team framed it thoughtfully, careful not to push too far, too fast. "This isn't something new," Hafida explained. "Mothers have always guided your children, shaped their futures. This is simply a way to continue that care by helping your children succeed in school." To both men and women, the message was the same: Participation wasn't rebellion; it was duty. Framed as an extension of motherhood, their responsibility to their children's education felt familiar, even natural. Still, questions followed privately from the women.

"But will our husbands agree?" one woman asked anxiously, her voice barely above a whisper.

"We will speak with them," Hafida assured her gently. She knew that for this idea to take root, it had to grow with the community, not against it.

Securing men's permission was essential to building trust and acceptance of women's new public roles. They spoke to husbands, fathers, and village elders, emphasizing that women's participation would strengthen families and improve children's futures.

Some men agreed because their leaders endorsed the idea; others followed their neighbors' example. A few had seen firsthand how small changes, like improved irrigation or new fuel-efficient cookstoves, had eased their daughters' workloads and made family life better. Over months, the hesitation began to soften. The idea no longer felt like a threat to tradition but an evolution of it.

By the end of that harvest season, PTAs were formed in several villages, each with an equal number of women and men. The first time a mother stood to speak, voice trembling but firm, something shifted in the air. It was no longer just about literacy or school attendance. It was about rewriting who got to speak for the community, and whose voices mattered. Within the PTAs, women began to shine. They contributed to school initiatives and received training in conflict resolution, financial literacy, and public speaking, skills that built their confidence and decision-making.

One parent, Aicha, shared with me her initial hesitation to join the PTA. "At the beginning, I didn't want to be a woman PTA leader because I didn't know how I could help my village. But after visiting Ouarzazate (the closest city) with other women from different villages, many things changed in my life and my way of thinking. Now I know I can bring many things to my community." During that visit, Aicha had the opportunity to connect with her peers, learn about their initiatives, hear how they went about the work, and understand the challenges they faced as women in leadership. Through these exchanges, she discovered how to find her own way.

Back in her village, Aicha took action. She organized after-school activities, weaving in Berber songs, games, and art to engage the children. The village began to buzz with new energy.

"Before, I was scared to speak with men," she told me one afternoon, her eyes bright with newfound confidence. "Now I'm determined to improve our school and encourage other women."

Change often begins quietly, with a few early adopters. When others see the difference it makes and the approval it earns, they start to follow. In Morocco, after two years, 98 percent of girls in the twenty-three villages were attending school.[3] Parents became so invested in this new norm that they began to complain to school administrators when teachers were absent and demanded additional staff when classrooms became overcrowded.

Sondré is a tiny village in Burkina Faso that rests in the vast, semi-arid Sahel, an unforgiving landscape at the front lines of climate change. To the north lies the endless reach of the Sahara; to the south, the dense green of tropical forest. The burnt, reddish sand of the Sahel stretches endlessly beneath a blazing sun. Days are searing, the heat unrelenting, temperatures hovering between 90 and 104 degrees Fahrenheit for eight months of the year. Without warning, sandstorms roll in, massive, opaque walls of moving earth that swallow the horizon. They arrive like a force of nature, enveloping everything in an abrasive, blinding cloud of fine grit, like a scene out of *Dune*. When the rain finally does come in July, it is brief and intense, covering the parched land with flash floods. Here, water is precious, more valuable than gold, as life is shaped by its scarcity.

Sondré is a maze of circular mud-and-straw huts clustered into compounds that house large extended families. At the heart of each compound lies a communal courtyard where the day's activities (cooking, weaving, tending animals) take place under the shade of a single tree or a makeshift awning. Most families are agropastoralists, herding livestock and cultivating millet and peanuts, relying on drip irrigation to make every drop of water count. Without electricity or running water, women and girls often walk miles to fetch water and firewood, their hands calloused from unforgiving daily labor.

Into this inhospitable environment arrived Mwangaza Action, a Burkinabe civil society group that aimed to end the deeply ingrained tradition of female genital mutilation/cutting (FGM/C). In Sondré, the group started by addressing the village's most immediate needs: repairing the broken water pump, as a way to build trust. For days, the villagers watched as the team worked, their curiosity mingling with skepticism. Then, when the pump sputtered to life, spitting out a stream of clear water, they cheered. The women, balancing heavy water jars on their heads, smiled for the first time in weeks.

From there, the changes came gradually, each one practical and tangible. Mwangaza Action introduced literacy classes under the shade of the lone baobab tree in the village center. Critically, it insisted on including women in all its efforts. Women bent over wooden benches, tracing unfamiliar letters on slates with chalk, their laughter mingling with the bleats of goats. A small health hut appeared next, offering basic medical care to villagers who had never dreamed of such access. With these improvements, the villagers' skepticism softened, replaced by cautious appreciation.

But trust alone wasn't enough. Mwangaza Action understood that to shift deeply rooted traditions, they would need the support of the village council, an assembly of elder men. These men were the keepers of tradition, and tradition left no room for women in leadership. But the tangible benefits of women's involvement—cleaner streets, healthier children, and more organized community efforts—spoke louder than words. So, when Fatoumata, a widow who attended the literacy classes, stood before the council to speak, "If women manage the health hut, we can make sure medicine is always available," her request was granted. Eventually, women began organizing cleanups, running the school, and taking on responsibilities previously unimagined. No longer confined to their homes, women were becoming central to community life. As perceptions shifted, so too did the future of girls and women, inching closer to a world where their rights and contributions were valued.

Sensing an opening, Mwangaza Action introduced the topic of addressing the entrenched practice of female genital mutilation/cutting. FGM/C was woven into the cultural fabric of Sondré, believed to preserve virginity, improve marriage prospects, and ensure social acceptance. For generations, mothers and grandmothers had carried out the practice, believing it was the best way to protect their daughters from social stigma. Yet it also caused great harm. Girls suffered infections, childbirth complications, and lifelong trauma. Also, the practice was rarely performed with the informed consent of the girl, making it a violation of her human rights.

Mwangaza Action approached the issue with the same respect that had earned the group the villagers' trust. Under the familiar baobab tree, they facilitated open dialogues, inviting men, women, and elders to speak. They framed the conversation not as a judgment of tradition, but as an exploration of its unintended consequences. Villagers began to grapple with the tension between their desire to protect their daughters and the harm caused by the ritual.

"We only want the best for our girls," one elder said during a gathering. "But if the best brings them suffering, then what do we do?" His words hung in the air, met by murmurs of agreement and the occasional nod. Mwangaza Action encouraged the villagers to reflect on their shared values: the deep love for their daughters and the collective desire to safeguard their futures.

Fatoumata, now a recognized leader in the community, spoke passionately during these sessions. "We can honor our daughters without harming them," she said one day, her voice steady and clear. Now that she held a firmer, more respected presence in the community, her words sparked further discussions in the courtyards and fields where women worked and in the shaded council meetings where men deliberated.

After another two years of steady progress, the village reached a turning point. One hot afternoon, as the sun baked the reddish sands, the villagers gathered in the central clearing for a public celebration. Dressed in vibrant fabrics, the women led the procession, their voices rising in song. The men followed, carrying banners that bore a simple but powerful message: FGM/C was no longer welcome in their community. This *public* declaration signified a *collective* decision that FGM/C was no longer acceptable. Just as in Morocco, where community consensus redefined girls' roles in education, in Sondré, it was the unity of the community—not isolated actions by individuals—that drove the change.

The experiences in Morocco and Burkina Faso reveal a crucial lesson: Building trust within communities and gaining the support of key gatekeepers are fundamental to creating a platform for change. When communities are engaged, and women actively involved in the conversation, it becomes possible to redefine what is acceptable. Grounding these discussions in shared values (like the desire to protect girls from harm) facilitates cultural transformation while preserving the community's sense of identity and cohesion.

Watching women and men in Morocco take small but courageous steps to reshape their daughters' futures moved me deeply. If it could happen there, in communities bound by tradition and scarcity, it can happen anywhere. Surely societies everywhere can learn to value women's economic choices as much as men's, to build a world where women can work safely, earn fair wages, and access the supports that make that possible: childcare, healthcare, and reproductive freedom.

The question, then, is not whether change is possible, but *how* do we make it happen. In Morocco, it began with allies, local leaders, parents, and teachers. The same must be true elsewhere. In refugee camps, in towns and cities around the world, influential gatekeepers, employers, community elders, and policymakers can set new expectations and model new norms. For example, Philadelphia joined Welcoming

America's Certified Welcoming program, a rigorous process that measures how inclusive a community truly is, from economic opportunity to civic participation. But what made it transformative wasn't just the certification; it was the coalition that emerged around it. City officials, immigrant-led organizations, faith groups, and local businesses came together under a shared vision: to make Philadelphia a place where every resident, no matter where they were born, could thrive. Volunteers hosted listening sessions in libraries and mosques. Small business owners mentored new arrivals. The mayor's office partnered with advocates to expand language access across departments so residents could navigate healthcare, housing, and public services without confusion.

When the city earned its Certified Welcoming designation, it wasn't just a badge, it was a declaration that belonging is a collective act. The process redefined leadership itself: Inclusion wasn't an afterthought but a measure of good governance. New norms took root through collaboration. Local leaders didn't wait for permission; they invited their neighbors to imagine a different kind of community, one where safety, opportunity, and dignity extended to all. Once people saw it was possible, they carried that idea forward.

We need that same courage everywhere. We must keep saying, loudly and unapologetically, that it is normal and right for refugee women to work, that hiring them is not an act of charity but a smart investment, and that including them in our workforce should not just be possible; it should be *expected*.

If we, as members of our own communities, have the power to define what is normal and acceptable, then we can also redefine it. I've seen it happen in a Massachusetts church that rallied to sponsor a refugee mother and her children from Afghanistan, providing housing, language lessons, and emotional care to help her rebuild her life. I've seen mentorship programs connect refugee women with industry professionals to restart their careers, and labor unions advocate for workplace safety laws that protect them.

PART 3

Collective Action

8

Solidarity

Allyship may be the first social idea that children today have to grapple with, long before they understand politics, inequality, or historical context. On playgrounds, in classrooms, and around dinner tables, kids are taught to be kind, to stand up for someone being teased, to include the child sitting alone. It feels simple, intuitive, a natural extension of what young children already understand: that all people deserve to feel safe, valued, and included. But as kids grow older, they notice that unfairness isn't always a bully on the playground. Sometimes it's built into the rules, embedded in the systems we inherit. It hides in who gets called on, who gets believed, whose families are welcome, whose stories are told. And that's when the idea of allyship, standing with those with fewer advantages, even when you're not the one being harmed, moves from kindness to courage.

On March 7, 1965, after peaceful marchers in Selma, Alabama, were clubbed and gassed after they crossed the Edmund Pettus Bridge, Martin Luther King Jr. issued a call, not just to Black Americans risking their lives for the right to vote, but to clergy, students, and people of conscience across the country. He asked them to come to Selma to march with them. And they came. Rabbis, priest, nuns, pastors, teachers, students, and ordinary citizens boarded buses and planes with the quiet understanding that their presence expanded the nation's moral imagination and reminded the country that injustice could not be someone else's problem. Some paid dearly for that choice. Reverend James Reeb, a white Unitarian minister answering King's call, was beaten by segregationists in Selma and died from his injuries. King embraced white allies, but he also challenged them. He warned that the greatest obstacle to equality were sympathetic observers who preferred order to justice. Progress required allies who would not merely feel bad about inequality, but who would act publicly, consistently, even at personal cost.

Decades later, the word *allyship* would take on new life. In the late 1970s, it emerged within the gay liberation movement to describe heterosexual supporters who stood with queer activists. By the 1990s and 2000s, universities and organizations adopted the term, searching for a way to describe what it means to challenge inequality from a position of relative advantage. As movements evolved, so did our understanding. Research and practice sharpened the definition: Allyship is not empathy alone, nor is it symbolic gestures or one-off protests; it is the ongoing, intentional act of using one's privilege, however small, to challenge structures that keep others at a disadvantage. It is a discipline, not an identity. Just like good health cannot be secured with a single bowl of fruit, justice cannot be secured with a single moment of solidarity. The idea of solidarity shifted from understanding the *what* to taking responsibility for the *how* to end oppression, especially when the harm does not directly affect you.

That *how* becomes easier to grasp when we look at the ecological patterns observed in species responding to climate change. In ecology, it is well established that organisms do not experience environmental stressors uniformly. Instead, their responses vary according to their biological traits, position within the ecosystem, and access to resources. These differential pressures produce distinct behavioral and physiological adaptations, none inherently superior, all shaped by context. Animals with stable habitats or plenty of resources often survive by making slower, smaller adjustments. They may change migration routes little by little or shift their breeding seasons. Their environment gives them space to act calmly and carefully. In contrast, animals living in places that are changing quickly, like coral reefs or melting ice regions, must respond with fast, dramatic actions. Coral may bleach suddenly, and mammals may flee their homes in large numbers. These behaviors might look extreme, but they are necessary for survival in harsh environments.

The same patterns appear in feminist movements. Women with privilege, such as legal protection, steady income, or strong social networks, can often speak out in ways that are polite, and gently push in ways that feel acceptable to those in power. Their social environment gives them safety to maneuver within its boundaries. But women who face poverty, racism, displacement, or constant risk don't win basic needs, such as schooling or housing, by being refined. They raise their voices, break expected rules, and persist despite exhaustion. These behaviors are not flaws. They are survival strategies shaped by real threats.

In science, we do not blame an animal for how it responds to climate stress. We do not call coral "overreactive" when it bleaches, and we do not say birds are "difficult" when they suddenly change migration patterns. Instead, we understand that they are reacting to pressures we may not see. Yet in social movements, women with more power sometimes judge the strategies of more vulnerable women. They may label them as angry, aggressive, or ungrateful. This misunderstanding can lead to exclusion or punishment, which repeats the same inequalities that the movement is meant to fight against.

Solidarity means recognizing that women do not all face the same conditions. They cannot all show up in the same way, and they should not have to. Just as in nature, different responses come from different pressures. There is no one acceptable way to dismantle injustice. Some of us will work from within the system, revising policies, reallocating resources, moving the levers of bureaucracy that turn slowly but surely. Others will stand outside those walls and push, in protest, in disruption, or in a collective refusal to play by rules that were never meant to include them. Movements are strongest not when we move in unison, but when we move in concert—many voices, many tactics, one purpose. Solidarity doesn't mean we all agree. It means we agree to help each other anyway. And this matters deeply when it comes to refugee women, for whom speaking up could mean detention, deportation, or disappearance.

We were sitting at a small café just off the main square in Rabat, the kind of place where the tables wobble slightly on the tiled floor and the ceiling fans stir the warm air.

My friend Samira and I had ordered atay, mint tea. Outside, motorbikes weaved through the crowds, and vendors called out prices for figs and olives. Inside, the smell of cardamom and tobacco lingered. Samira cupped her glass between both hands, staring into the swirl, and asked quietly, "You heard about Fadoua, right?" I shook my head no. She leaned closer. It was 2011. Fadoua was twenty-five, a single mother raising two children in a shantytown outside Souk Sebt Ouled Nemma. The Cities Without Slums project aimed to improve urban conditions for people like Fadoua, by relocating slum dwellers to better housing through upgrading, rehousing, and resettlement programs. Most families had been given land and housing support to rebuild—not Fadoua. As an unmarried, single mother, she could not legally be a head of household. So, when they tore down her little makeshift shelter, she had nothing left, no home, land, or rights to claim. Samira sighed, a long, slow breath. "They pushed her so far to the edge that there was nowhere left to stand. Imagine being told your children don't count because you're a woman raising them alone."

The café around us buzzed with small conversations. "One morning," Samira continued, "Fadoua went to the town hall. People thought she was there to plead her case, again. Instead, she poured flammable liquid over herself and set her body on fire." Samira swallowed, eyes fixed on the table. "Her last words were, 'They destroyed my shack and called me crazy. Where do I go now? I have nowhere to go.'"

Samira's story pressed into the space between us. As I sipped the last of my atay, Hélène came to mind. We met that same year. Hélène lived thousands of miles to the south, in Côte d'Ivoire, where she had spent twenty years tending a small plot of land, coaxing a living from the soil, raising eight children on what it provided. When her husband died, custom dictated that the land be handed over to his extended family. Overnight, the fields she had cared for became forbidden ground. And she, like Fadoua, was left with the same devastating question: "Where do I go now?"

I shared this with Samira, and she nodded absently. Stories like theirs reveal a pattern far larger than two women's lives. In much of Africa, where nearly 90 percent of wealth is tied to land, fewer than one in ten women owns any.[1] Globally, the number is fewer than one in five.[2] Land is never just land. It is economic security, stability, and identity, a place to stand in the world. Losing it doesn't only take income; it takes dignity, independence, and the sense that tomorrow is still possible.

But beneath the statistics lies something even deeper: a quiet, pervasive devaluing of women. For Hélène and Fadoua, the loss was not only economic; it was communal. In societies where land defines belonging and property anchors kinship and social recognition, being denied land is often a signal that one does not fully belong. In agrarian and semi-agrarian communities, land rights determine participation in local councils, entry into communal decision-making, access to shared resources like water or grazing, and eligibility for collective compensation or state subsidies.

Women without land are often treated as dependents rather than stakeholders. They are excluded from the webs of reciprocity that sustain families and communities: labor sharing during harvest, mutual aid in crises, or the support of neighbors and elders when disaster strikes. Without these ties, women are isolated. They have no one to advocate for them, amplify their voices, or stand beside them as their homes crumble.

For Fadoua and Hélène, there was no one to catch them when everything fell apart. Their stories, shared over tea, did not feel exceptional. They revealed a structural truth: Without land, women are often cut off from both economic security and the informal social safety nets that make survival possible.

In a quiet village in central Morocco, I sat on the floor in Manal's home. The space was humble and inviting, the walls painted in warm, earthy tones reminiscent of the Saharan sands. Handwoven rugs in deep reds and oranges adorned the floor, adding vibrancy to the cool, elongated room. The room's proportions created an open yet intimate atmosphere, perfectly suited for the gathering already in progress.

A group of women sat cross-legged on the floor around me, wearing djellabas—loose, hooded caftans draped over their clothes to shield them from dirt and sand. Their expressions held a mix of exhaustion and determination, their weathered hands and dust-covered clothes revealing lives shaped by hard labor. These women, spanning generations from age twenty-five to seventy-three, belonged to the Soulaliyates—Berber tribes who live on land that is held collectively rather than owned privately. Their territory belongs to the tribe as a whole. Individual families are assigned plots to farm, but they do not hold title deeds and cannot sell the land. It is managed under shared rules, with elders overseeing its use. Each family cultivates its own section, yet ownership remains communal.

I first met Manal in 2008 through my friend Khadija from the Democratic Association of Moroccan Women (ADFM), a women's rights organization established in 1985.

Like many rural women in Morocco, Manal's life revolved around the farm, working the fields, collecting firewood, and tending cattle. Her days followed the pattern of generations before her, predictable and labor-intensive with one exception: Tuesdays and Thursdays.

Those brief departures from routine were the earliest signs that the ground beneath her community was beginning to shift. The year before, in 2007, the Moroccan government had begun selling off tribal lands—nearly half the country's territory—to private and public real estate developers. According to tribal law, only men could inherit or benefit from communal land sales. For women like Manal, and for the women gathered in her home that day, the impact of that law was profound. They had grown up together, worked side by side, shared meals, and cared for one another through sickness and harvests. Now many of them, especially those unmarried, widowed, or divorced, faced displacement and destitution as the land sales uprooted their lives. Some women were pushed into urban slums, forced to live in shacks under punishing conditions. For them, the stakes were painfully clear: Act or lose everything.

By the time I sat with them in 2008, they had already spent a year fighting for change. Their twice-weekly protests, held every Tuesday and Thursday, had become a consistent force, and Manal had recently formed a partnership with ADFM.

The room buzzed with overlapping voices, each woman's indignation fueling the next. "Our men are dominated by selfishness," one fumed. "This situation has nothing to do with tradition; it is . . . their greed." Another woman retorted: "A woman with no children lived with her husband. His children from a first marriage threw her away when he died. Now she lives in a shantytown."

Their indignation swelled like a wave. "A brother gains billions while his sister can hardly afford her needs or find work as a farm laborer," another woman offered, her voice trembling with rage. "How can a man live in a large house while his sister lives in a slum?"

These women had spent their lives working the land, contributing to their families and fulfilling their roles under the social contract. Yet as the land was sold, their futures became precarious, dependent entirely on the decisions of male heads of household. Would these men include their female relatives or abandon them to start new lives elsewhere?

It was this uncertainty that forced women to act. Starting in 2007, they drew inspiration from the Soulaliyate women 250 miles to the east, who had begun their fight for land rights back in 2000. Stepping beyond their traditional roles as caretakers, they turned to the only authority that could challenge tribal law: the government.

Manal began gathering her female neighbors twice a week, organizing them to ride into town and join other Soulaliyate women in peaceful protest. Together, they converged at the town hall, their voices rising in unison with a rallying chant: *One foot up, one foot down. For my land, my blood will shed.*

For these women, entering the public sphere was a daunting and radical act. Their lives had long been confined to the home and the fields, and this newfound visibility came with a price. Manal endured mockery from neighbors who accused her of defying tradition, insults from men in the community, and relentless intimidation at home from her husband. Many women faced worse: Some were physically assaulted at protests by jeering men.

The risks stretched far beyond harassment. If the Soulaliyate women lost the support of a brother, angered a husband, or were seen as competing with a son or uncle over land rights, they could end up destitute. They had no wealth, privilege, or safety net to cushion them if they fell. Yet this only made their persistence convey a more powerful message: *We won't stop, no matter the cost.*

Fortunately, the Soulaliyate women didn't stand alone. Their most powerful ally arrived not from within their villages but from the cities, an unexpected partnership with ADFM. On the surface, the two groups could not have been more different. ADFM's members were mostly urban Arab women; the Soulaliyate women were rural Berber farmers. Rural Berbers often saw urban Arabs as morally lax and disconnected from the land, while Arabs sometimes dismissed Berbers as backward or unsophisticated. History, language, and geography had long kept them worlds apart.

And yet, when the land sales began stripping Soulaliyate women of their rights, ADFM stepped in to help. ADFM women were not personally affected by the communal land crisis. They were not at risk of losing their homes or property overnight. But they recognized the shared purpose in dismantling injustice in a legal system that discriminated against women. "Our expertise is in training these women to become leaders and spokespeople," my friend Khadija told me. "We help them articulate their demands and engage directly in advocacy." ADFM's allyship was practical, sustained, and grounded in the Soulaliyate women's actual needs.

They taught women land management law, governance, and public speaking; they helped them navigate the bureaucracy. They also pushed from the top, lobbying national policymakers, invoking international legal frameworks like the Convention on the Elimination of All Forms of Discrimination Against Women, to which Morocco was a signatory, to push for equality in land ownership, property rights, and compensation. What emerged was a shared model of collective, collaborative leadership rooted in care. Women didn't seek power over others but power *with* them.

Over the years, the Soulaliyate protests grew larger, bolder, and impossible to ignore. Their persistence transformed policy. The Ministry of Interior eventually issued a bulletin granting women equal rights to communal land revenues. A state-run lottery followed, distributing more than 860 land plots[3] equally between men and women. Still, the women pressed forward.

In 2018, they won another groundbreaking victory: the right to full market value compensation in future land sales. The push came after uncovering exploitative deals, like one in Aoulad Sbita, where male representatives sold eight hundred hectares of communal land for fifty dirhams per hectare to a private developer. The company flipped it for 2,500 dirhams per hectare, profiting fifty-fold while the community received scraps. The victory came with complexities. Attitudes toward protesting women shifted when men began to benefit financially from women's efforts, such as through higher market returns on land sales. It revealed how women's gains are often accepted only when they align with patriarchal interests.

Then, the collaboration between ADFM and the Soulaliyate activists led to something historic: the 2019 amendment of the 1919 Dahir, granting women equal rights in land ownership and management. A landmark win not only for Berber women but for all Moroccan women.

Through these stories, I've come to realize that solidarity requires humility, courage, and steadfastness. Climate scientists tell us that species survive upheaval not by clinging to old hierarchies but by adapting—by changing behaviors, forming new networks of cooperation, and redistributing effort in ways that strengthen the whole habitat. Solidarity asks us to do the same. When we step forward from positions of privilege (unearned advantages, opportunities, and resources due to social identity), the point is not to direct but to adjust our actions to meet the needs of those living closest to harm by redistributing resources and opportunities and strengthening the habitat or systems we live in. Lasting change grows from grassroots movements rooted in mutual respect. As allies, our first responsibility is to cultivate genuine relationships, connections resilient enough to hold under pressure.

At the same time, it is crucial to recognize the risks inherent in challenging entrenched power. Whenever women seek to disrupt or reweave power and resources, backlash is inevitable. Upending power relations triggers resistance from those who benefit from the status quo—sometimes men, sometimes women—who may resort to emotional, economic, verbal, or physical abuse; destruction of property; withholding of wages or rights; or denial of access to services, all to protect culturally sanctioned hierarchies.

True solidarity recognizes both realities: It is active, consistent, and adaptable, and it requires preparing for backlash while staying committed to justice.

9

The Butterfly Effect

In the early 1960s, Edward Lorenz, a meteorologist and mathematician at MIT, theorized that he could use mathematical equations to predict the weather days or even weeks in advance. Although computers at the time were clunky and slow, they were capable of handling the repetitive calculations required. Using one of these machines, Lorenz built a simple weather model and ran a simulation. He typed in a sequence of numbers—temperatures, air pressure, wind speeds—but to save space, in one of these tests he rounded the numbers off slightly. For example, instead of using 0.506127, he entered 0.506, a tiny, almost unnoticeable difference.

When the simulation finished, Lorenz was puzzled. The weather patterns it predicted did not align with the original model at all. At first, he thought the computer had made a mistake. He rechecked everything, no errors. That's when it hit him: The tiny change in the initial numbers, less than one-thousandth, had caused the entire weather system to behave differently.

A seemingly small and insignificant change can cause

a drastic shift. Lorenz likened it to the flap of a butterfly's wings in Brazil leading to a tornado in Texas weeks later, a phenomenon later called the butterfly effect.

There is a similar feeling working with refugee women. You don't often see the immediate impact of efforts like advocating for girls' education, teaching financial literacy, pushing for salary transparency, or calling out sexual harassment, but when you zoom out and look miles down the road or years into the future, the impact becomes clear: Every action grows in scale and significance as it ripples outward, no matter how small.

For displaced people, small personal changes like a new skill, increased freedom of movement, or a community role can unlock transformative potential. In claiming more freedoms or resources, women step outside traditional roles and responsibilities ascribed to their gender. To claim these rights, they move from the privacy of the home into public spaces and roles. This seemingly modest acceleration crests into a wave, at which point women are better positioned to challenge entrenched societal norms and tackle systemic inequalities.

This can lead to tangible community-wide improvements: better systems, improved services, fairer distribution of resources, safer environments, greater economic opportunities, and enhanced community participation. The key difference is one butterfly flapping its wings is rarely enough. It takes a group, working collectively, to generate the momentum needed to overturn deeply rooted social expectations.

Sometimes, meaningful change doesn't come from solving the big problem all at once, but from chipping away at it. It's the gradual, persistent efforts, the hard conversations, the small policy shifts, the mentoring of future leaders, that begin to move the needle, so that others can continue the work. Real change is built this way—compounded, collective, and enduring.

I've seen the butterfly effect in action. It was in 2022. I found myself once again with my old friend Abdelkhalk. He was in his fifties now, a little more silver in his hair, but with the same boundless energy that kept him working with villagers long after many others had stepped away. We talked about our days in Ouarzazate and the mountains. Little Rashida wasn't little anymore. At twenty-two, she was the primary school teacher of her village.

Years earlier, Rashida's grandmother, Malika, boarded a bus for the first time. She headed to the local administration office to submit a scholarship application so her granddaughter could attend high school in the nearby town. What looked like routine paperwork was in fact the first flap of a butterfly's wing. The scholarship allowed Rashida to continue her education. When she returned home from high school, she organized literacy classes for the women of Timicha Toundoute, her own mother and grandmother among them. She coordinated summer programs for children from neighboring communities, creating opportunities she herself had once wanted. Eventually, she ran for local office and won.

Rashida's path was part of a pattern. Sixty-two miles east of Ouarzazate, in the village of Tamezrite N'Ait Affane, another story had unfolded. Darifa, a childless widow in her fifties, had endured a lifetime of adversity. Illiterate, landless, and without a formal position in her subsistence-farming village, she had lived on its margins.

Yet invisibility never quite fit her. She was cheerful and talkative, with a quick humor and boisterous laugh. When her husband died, her neighbors looked after her in turns, offering a roof and food.

The PTA in Tamezrite N'Ait Affane became her vocation. She was the first woman to volunteer to join. "I know every child in the village," she said. "They're all my family."

We met in 2007 when she strode into the project office in Ouarzazate and instantly commanded the room. Sitting across from me, she rested her elbows firmly on the table, and declared, "I am Darifa, a woman leader with the Parent-Teacher Association of Tamezrite N'Ait Affane. What do you want to know about my community?"

Darifa wasn't just a participant; she was a force. She trained other women in the mechanics of being heard. She showed them how to lean forward, place their arms on the table, hold eye contact, and raise their voices when interrupted. "This is how you make men listen," she told them, a mischievous spark in her eyes. And gradually, they did. The village imam later acknowledged, "At first, the women were timid. They didn't talk. Now they have a lot to say. And we men, we listen."

Through the PTA, Darifa came to understand the broader value of education not just for children, but for herself. She enrolled in literacy classes, and with every word she learned to read and write, she gained more awareness of her rights. Before long, another wing flapped as other women joined her.

For six years, the women of Tamezrite N'Ait Affane transformed girls' education. And then, one day, Darifa and five other women stepped out into the cold, crisp morning of the High Atlas Mountains. The moon cast a soft blue light on the winding path. Each woman had risen hours earlier to prepare breakfast and tea for their families. The smell of mint lingered in their kitchens as they quietly left home, careful not to wake anyone. Wrapped in their finest haiks or wearing djellabas embroidered with bright, intricate motifs, they seemed out of place in the rugged, dry mountain landscape. The dirt paths they treaded snaked down steep, rocky slopes; only their lighthearted chatter broke the stillness of the predawn.

For two and a half hours they walked, voices rising and falling as they gossiped. When they reached the road, the first pink light of day stretched across the horizon. They stood waiting for the bus that would carry them to the city of Ouarzazate, the capital of the province. Their destination: the governor's office.

From their literacy teacher, the women had learned about Morocco's 2004 Family Code, a groundbreaking reform that promised greater rights for women. But in their village almost ten years later, these promises had remained unfulfilled. The women were determined to make their concerns known, to explain how the Family Code was being ignored, and to demand its fair implementation in their community.

When they finally arrived in the city, the bustling streets were alive with activity: the clatter of carts, the sharp cries of vendors, the hum of traffic. The women, dusty from the road, approached the imposing iron gate of the governor's compound. Armed guards strode forward, blocking their way.

"Do you have an appointment?" one guard asked gruffly.

"No, but we must speak with the governor," Darifa replied.

The guards dismissed the women with a wave. "Come back another time. You can't enter without permission."

The women did not retreat. "We've come too far to leave now." Darifa moved closer to the gate. Her companions joined her, and they reprimanded the guards for treating their sisters and mothers in such a manner. Passersby began to notice, murmuring among themselves as the scene unfolded.

After an hour under the searing sun, a junior official appeared, clipboard in hand, his expression stern. "What is it you want?" he asked.

Darifa spoke with conviction: They were there to speak with the governor, no one else. The official hesitated, but finally the women were led inside the gates, into the cool sanctuary of the courtyard. There, the noise of the city faded away, replaced by the gentle trickle of a fountain at the courtyard's center. The courtyard was a masterpiece of Moroccan craftsmanship, with Zellige tiles in vibrant geometric patterns, ornate woodwork arches framing the space, and the fragrance of citrus trees and flowers hanging in the air.

The women waited for hours, sitting on a stone bench under the trees. Around them, visitors came and went, some whispering furtively to mid-level bureaucrats, others slipping bribes into eager hands. Darifa and the women had neither connections nor money.

Finally, as the afternoon sun began to dip, they were summoned into the governor's office. The room was cavernous, its walls adorned with ceiling-high portraits of the king and the royal family. The governor sat behind a vast desk, flanked by aides, and asked the women to sit around a long conference table.

The women explained why they had come. Ten years into the passage of the new Family Code, girls as young as fifteen in their village were still being married off, women were being abandoned by husbands without support, and decisions were being made without wives' consent. The women's voices grew stronger as they spoke.

The governor leaned back in his chair, studying the group before him. Then, without a word, he picked up the phone. "Send for the delegate of social affairs," he said to the person at the other end of the line. "There is a community here with questions. They must be answered." He looked at Darifa. "You will have your meeting."

A month later, officials arrived in Tamezrite N'Ait Affane. They held a town hall meeting, outlining the provisions of the Family Code and explaining how to report violations. For the women, it was a tangible victory—evidence that a single, courageous action could prompt a response. Each step they took pushed against long-standing gender roles, small disruptions accumulating over time. These flutters gradually began to reshape the norms that had constrained women and girls for generations.

For refugees immense consequences can arise from the beat of a wing.

In September 2015, the body of Alan Kurdi, a three-year-old Syrian boy, washed up on the Turkish shoreline. His family had been fleeing the civil war in Syria. In Turkey, they boarded an overcrowded inflatable boat bound for the Greek island of Kos. Minutes after departing, the boat capsized. Alan, his five-year-old brother, Ghalib, and their mother, Rehanna, drowned.

Their story might have remained unknown were it not for a single photograph taken by a journalist: Alan lying face down on the beach. The image was stark and impossible to ignore. It spread rapidly around the world, forcing global attention onto the human cost of the refugee crisis.

What followed demonstrated the butterfly effect. One image set off a chain reaction—public debate, protests, and policy discussions. In Europe, it helped shift public sentiment, with Germany accepting more than a million Syrian asylum seekers. In response to the global outcry, hundreds of companies across multiple countries committed to hiring nearly a quarter-million refugees, offering jobs and the possibility of rebuilding stable lives.

Alan Kurdi's death sparked a worldwide call to welcome refugees. But it doesn't have to take a tragedy to compel action. Change can begin with something simpler: volunteer or mentor, host social gatherings that connect friends with newcomers, and support women-owned refugee businesses. When we see them as part of our shared community, we are more likely to act with empathy, and with the urgency their circumstances demand.

Off the coast of Lanzarote in Spain's Canary Islands, twelve to fifteen meters below the water's surface, rests a world of stone. Three hundred human figures frozen mid-stride, form Jason deCaires Taylor's *Museo Atlántico*. At its center is the Raft of Lampedusa: an inflatable raft crowded with refugees, a memorial to the thousands who have risked everything to cross the Mediterranean in search of safety.

Suspended in the quiet blue, these figures appear abandoned, untouched, unrescued, echoing the reality faced by too many displaced people today.

The installation captures the impossible choices that define forced migration. It compels us to acknowledge that their fate is not inevitable. We are not mere witnesses to this story. We have the collective capacity to shape a different pathway, one that safeguards lives, extends dignity, and strengthens the communities we share.

Yes, refugee women arrive in new countries with no safety net, no map, and often no margin for error. They step into unfamiliar streets living in the shadow of war, loss, and impossible expectations, while navigating gender roles that shift overnight. They have no plan B, which means every choice becomes a calculus of survival, and earning an income means balancing opportunity against danger.

And yet, across continents and cultures, refugee women invent ways to minimize risk in circumstances that would break most of us. Research and lived experience tell the same story: The single greatest determinant of economic success for displaced women is a strong social network. When women find or build community, they create a safety net where none existed. They become each other's childcare, job leads, crisis responders, translators, and advocates. These networks are lifelines. And still the world mistakes women's resilience for evidence that they need less support, rather than more.

But the real barrier is not women. It is the system.

Women earn less because they are women. Refugee women earn even less because multiple biases collide: racism, sexism, classism, and cultural stereotypes. We devalue women's contributions—emotionally, socially, economically—and then act surprised when they struggle to advance.

Power lives in social hierarchies, and those hierarchies teach us, quietly and persistently, to accept less than we deserve. Legal and economic structures uphold this arrangement, dividing women from one another and splintering movements that should be unstoppable. Too often, the women with the most privilege are elevated as the face of progress, while those with the least—refugee women, undocumented women, women of color, poor women—are left to navigate danger alone.

That is why access to policies and services is essential. Childcare, healthcare, safe transportation, legal pathways to work; these are not mere supports but scaffolding that creates possibility. They transform the landscape of what a woman can choose, and who she can become.

And the good news is that norms that define what she can become can change. They always have. They change when communities decide to rewrite the rules. They change through collective effort, through allies who take risks, through women who refuse to wait for permission. They change when people choose justice over tradition, courage over comfort.

But solidarity is not about centering ourselves. It is not about speaking for others. It is about standing with those who have the least privilege and following their lead. The movement rises when those at the margins rise.

The impact of this work ripples outward. One woman accessing a safe job changes a household. A network of women changes a neighborhood. A community that embraces refugee women transforms a city.

And so, here is my truth that I want to leave you with: We have power. Collective, formidable, world-shaping power.

Let's use it, not softly, not conditionally, not only when it's convenient. Let's use it so that the most vulnerable among us are never left behind. Let's use it to lift every boat, especially the ones most battered by the storm.

We are called to rise.

And none of us rises alone.

Acknowledgments

This whole adventure began with an email from the wonderful team at Pivotal Ventures—and somehow snowballed into . . . well, *this*. Along the way, I had an army of helpers, encouragers, and general firekeepers.

First, to my endlessly supportive husband, Georg, who believed in me, occasionally reminded me that "taking a break" is not a sign of weakness, and helped me carve out space to write this work by taking on more responsibility. To my children, who made sure I didn't take myself too seriously, offering me the gift of time and space to write this book and bringing a humor that diminished the seriousness of it. That gift often came at the cost of missed soccer games, skipped Friday movie nights, and late-night homework marathons.

Ada Williams Prince, thank you for opening the door for me to write this book—just as you have opened doors for so many other women of color in leadership—and for believing, and persuading me, that I could do it. Sussan Khozouri for reading my very first proposal, offering support so I didn't feel alone. Lise Funderberg, who pushed this book forward, working these pages over and over again with me, patiently accompanying me along the way.

Will Schwalbe, my publisher, who refused to let me quit,

even when the path ahead felt as uncertain as a GPS that keeps recalculating. Stephanie Cabot, my agent, for steadily guiding me with a kind and unshakable clarity through my first publishing rodeo. Lee Oglesby and Julianna Haubner, my editors at Flatiron, whose sharp eyes and analytical minds made every page stronger. To my friends who kept asking, "How is the book coming along?" The answer: "It's done now!"

Finally, to the countless refugee women, and to my humanitarian and development colleagues, who have shown me what strength, tenacity, and the power of a fair shot truly look like, your courage and resolve continue to light the way.

Resources for Further Learning

The following organizations, publications, and media offer in-depth research, data, and storytelling on women refugees and their economic lives.

ORGANIZATIONS AND THINK TANKS

- **Migration Policy Institute.** Research and policy analysis on global migration, including gender dimensions in refugee livelihoods.
- **Overseas Development Institute (ODI).** Development research institute producing reports on displacement, humanitarian aid, and gendered economic participation.
- **Witwatersrand University—African Centre for Migration and Society.** Africa's leading academic center on migration studies, with work on forced displacement and gender.
- **Institute for Women's Policy Research (IWPR).** Focuses on women's economic equity, with some studies intersecting migration and displacement.
- **Center for Global Development (CGD).** Economic research think tank with reports on forced migration and women's labor market outcomes.

KEY ACADEMIC AND RESEARCH SOURCES

- **UNHCR—Global Trends Reports and Thematic Studies.** Annual data and thematic reports, including *Women, Work, and War: Syrian Women in the Refugee Crisis*.
- **Women's Refugee Commission (WRC).** Notably, the WRC's *Preventing Gender-Based Violence, Building Livelihoods* (2011) explores how to reduce risk of GBV in economic programs. Read the report at https://www.womensrefugeecommission.org/research-resources/preventing-gender-based-violence-building-livelihoods-guidance-and-tools-for-improved-programming/.
- **World Bank—"Gender and Forced Displacement."** Examines how gender affects refugee labor market integration.
- **Forced Migration Review (FMR).** Open-access academic journal with special issues on "Economics of Displacement" and "Gender and Displacement."
- **Journal of Refugee Studies.** Peer-reviewed, interdisciplinary scholarship blending economics, sociology, and anthropology.

NGO AND POLICY REPORTS

- **CARE International.** *Women's Economic Empowerment in Crisis Settings*, featuring case studies of refugee women in business and formal labor markets.
- **Oxfam.** Research on gendered economic impacts of displacement, particularly in Lebanon, Jordan, and Bangladesh.
- **International Labour Organization (ILO).** *Employment of Syrian Refugees* and *Women at Work in Crisis Settings*, covering labor rights, informal work, and policy frameworks.
- **Pasos Prohibidos.** A multimedia investigative report on migrant and refugee journeys. View the report at https://migrantes-otro-mundo.elclip.org/pasos-prohibidos.html.

MULTIMEDIA AND STORYTELLING

- **Refugees Deeply (archive).** Policy-focused journalism interwoven with personal narratives.
- **Podcasts:**
    * *The Refugee Experience*. Interviews with women entrepreneurs in refugee camps.
    * *Displaced*. Hosted by Grant Gordon and Ravi Gurumurthy (IRC), featuring in-depth discussions with humanitarian leaders.
    * *Forced to Flee* (UNHCR). Oral histories from people displaced over the past seventy years.
    * *The Wait* (*The Guardian*). Five-part narrative on refugees in Indonesia facing legal limbo.
    * *Rethinking Humanitarianism* (*The New Humanitarian*). Critical discussions on humanitarian reform, with a focus on equity.
    * *What's Unsaid* (*The New Humanitarian*). Conversations on conflicts and humanitarian issues.
    * *Resettled* (VPM). Stories from newly resettled refugees in Virginia.
    * *Integrate That!*. Perspectives from forcibly displaced people in the UK and Europe.
    * *Not Really Strangers.* Exploring the refugee experience.

DATA PORTALS

- **UNHCR Data Portal.** Searchable datasets, with filters for gender and livelihoods.
- **World Bank Gender Data Portal.** Global gender-disaggregated statistics, including forced migration contexts.
- **ILOstat.** Labor market statistics for refugees in host countries.

Notes

CHAPTER 1: UPENDED GENDER NORMS

1. "One in Three Women Experiences Gender-Based Violence," UN News, November 15, 2024, https://news.un.org/en/story/2024/11/1157046. Accessed January 8, 2026.
2. Eliya M. Zulu et al., "Overview of Migration, Poverty and Health Dynamics in Nairobi City's Slum Settlements," *Journal of Urban Health: Bulletin of the New York Academy of Medicine* 88, suppl. 2 (June 29, 2011): 185–99, https://pmc.ncbi.nlm.nih.gov/articles/PMC3132239/.
3. "Do All Refugees Live in Camps?" USA for UNHCR, https://www.unrefugees.org/refugee-facts/camps/.
4. Thomas Ginn, Reva Resstack, and Helen Dempster, "Refugees' Work Rights Around the World: Introducing Our New Report," *Center for Global Development* (blog), July 28, 2022, https://www.cgdev.org/blog/refugees-work-rights-around-world-introducing-our-new-report.
5. United States Department of State, "Country Reports on Human Rights Practices for 2010: Ethiopia," Bureau of Democracy, Human Rights, and Labor, April 8, 2011, https://2009-2017.state.gov/j/drl/rls/hrrpt/2010/af/154346.htm. Accessed January 8, 2026.
6. UNHCR Kenya and Kenya Department of Refugee Services, *Kenya Statistics Package—28 February 2025*, UNHCR Kenya report, February 28, 2025, https://www.unhcr.org/ke/media/kenya-statistics-package-28-february-2025-pdf.

7. United Nations Office for the Coordination of Humanitarian Affairs, *Syrian Arab Republic 2022*, Financial Tracking Service, last modified 2022, https://fts.unocha.org/countries/218/summary/2022.
8. Human Rights Watch, "Syria: Events of 2020," *World Report 2021*, https://www.hrw.org/world-report/2021/country-chapters/syria.
9. "Ukraine War Hits Africa's Most Vulnerable as Aid Costs Spike," Reuters, May 30, 2022.
10. International Monetary Fund, "Five Things to Know About the Informal Economy," IMF Country Focus, July 28, 2021, https://www.imf.org/en/News/Articles/2021/07/28/na-072821-five-things-to-know-about-the-informal-economy.
11. United Nations High Commissioner for Refugees, "UNHCR Study Shows Rapid Deterioration in Living Conditions of Syrian Refugees in Jordan," January 14, 2015, https://www.unhcr.org/us/news/news-releases/unhcr-study-shows-rapid-deterioration-living-conditions-syrian-refugees-jordan.
12. 3RP Joint Secretariat (UNHCR and UNDP), *Regional Refugee and Resilience Plan (3RP): Regional Strategic Overview 2021–2022*, December 2020, ALNAP help library, https://www.3rpsyriacrisis.org/portfolio/rso2021_2022/.
13. 3RP Joint Secretariat (UNHCR and UNDP), *Regional Refugee and Resilience Plan (3RP): Regional Strategic Overview 2021–2022*.
14. Norwegian Refugee Council, "What You Need to Know About Syrian Child Marriage," October 10, 2019, https://www.nrc.no/perspectives/2019/what-you-need-to-know-about-syrian-child-marriage.

CHAPTER 2: EVERYDAY RISK

1. United Nations Office for the Coordination of Humanitarian Affairs, *Global Humanitarian Overview 2024: Global Achievements*, OCHA report, December 2023.
2. Diana J. Arango, Jocelyn Kelly, Jeni Klugman, and Elena Ortiz, "Forced Displacement and Violence Against Women: A Policy Brief," Gender Dimensions of Forced Displacement, World Bank

Group, December 2021, https://documents1.worldbank.org/curated/en/593151638940044686/pdf/Forced-Displacement-and-Violence-Against-Women-A-Policy-Brief.pdf.

3. United Nations Women, "Facts and Figures: Humanitarian Action," retrieved July 17, 2025, https://www.unwomen.org/en/what-we-do/humanitarian-action/facts-and-figures#:~:text=View%20infographic%20%C2%BB,by%20natural%20disasters%20%5B5%5D.
4. Australian Science Media Centre, "The Rate of Violence Against Women Has Barely Changed in 25 Years," SciMEX, November 20, 2025, https://www.scimex.org/newsfeed/the-rate-of-violence-against-women-has-barely-changed-in-25-years. Accessed January 8, 2026.
5. Atalay Rediet, Girma Ayele, Saba Clarke, and Miriam Michael, "The Quarantine Paradox: The Economic Cost of the Increase in Violence Against Women and Girls in Sub-Saharan Africa," *Frontiers in Public Health* 10 (November 9, 2022), https://doi.org/10.3389/fpubh.2022.1029823.
6. "Falling Short? Humanitarian Funding and Reform," Development Initiatives, October 2024, p. 6, https://devinit.org/resources/falling-short-humanitarian-funding-reform/executive-summary/#downloads.
7. Sona Martirosyan, "Sexual Harassment in the Workplace in Armenia," JAMnews, April 3, 2023, https://jam-news.net/sexual-harassment-in-armenia/.
8. Alexander Betts, Naohiko Omata, and Olivier Sterck, "Refugee Economies in Kenya," Refugee Studies Centre, University of Oxford, February 2018, https://www.rsc.ox.ac.uk/files/files-1/refugee-economies-report-web.pdf.
9. "Small Hands, Enormous Commitments: Child Labour Among Syrian Refugee Children in Lebanon," *Euro-Mediterranean Human Rights Monitor*, October 13, 2017, https://euromedmonitor.org/en/article/2101/Small-hands-enormous-commitments-Child-labour-among-Syrian-refugee-children-in-Lebanon.%20time.com+6.

10. "Influx of Refugees and Limited Firewood Leads to Spike in Gender-Based Violence," Women's Refugee Commission, January 6, 2016, www.womensrefugeecommission.org/blog/influx-of-refugees-and-limited-firewood-leads-to-spike-in-gender-based-violence/.

CHAPTER 3: THE BOOTSTRAP MYTH

1. Samuel J. Abrams, "The US Still Believes in Hard Work and Upward Mobility," American Enterprise Institute, February 24, 2021, https://www.aei.org/op-eds/the-us-still-believes-in-hard-work-and-upward-mobility.
2. "An Overview of America's Working Poor," Data in Action series, PolicyLink, n.d., https://www.policylink.org/data-in-action/overview-america-working-poor.
3. Statista Research Department, "Poverty Rate in the United States in 2023, by Age and Gender," Statista, 2025, https://www.statista.com/statistics/233154/us-poverty-rate-by-gender/.
4. Jeanne Batalova, "College-Educated Immigrants in the United States," Migration Policy Institute, September 12, 2024, https://www.migrationpolicy.org/article/college-educated-immigrants-united-states.
5. *Poverty Myths and Stereotypes*, fact sheet, Just Harvest/Action Against Hunger, January 2015, https://dougslangandlit.blog/wp-content/uploads/2021/03/just-harvest-poverty-myths-stereotypes-fact-sheet.pdf.
6. Eliza Daley, "Women in Agriculture," Resilience.org, March 8, 2023, https://www.resilience.org/stories/2023-03-08/women-in-agriculture/.
7. Jessica Shao and Yoolim Lee, "Gender Norms and Women's Double Burden in East Asia," *Diplomat*, November 29, 2023, https://thediplomat.com/2023/11/gender-norms-and-womens-double-burden-in-east-asia/.
8. Oxfam International, "Not All Gaps Are Created Equal: The True Value of Care Work," January 14, 2020, https://www.oxfam.org/en/not-all-gaps-are-created-equal-true-value-care-work.

9. Kate Carroll, *Not Ready, Still Waiting: Governments Have a Long Way to Go in Preparing to Address Gender Inequality and the SDGs*, ActionAid UK report, September 1, 2016, https://www.actionaid.org.uk/publications/not-ready-still-waiting.
10. Bruce Horovitz, "More than 60% Say Caregiving Increased Their Level of Stress and Worry, New AARP Report Finds," AARP, November 1, 2023, www.aarp.org/caregiving/medical/report-caregiver-mental-health/#:~:text=Daily%20caregiving%20challenges,or%20grandchildren%20in%20their%20home.
11. "Working Families," First Five Years Fund, 2025, https://www.ffyf.org/by-topic/working-families/.
12. "This Is How Much Child Care Costs in 2023," *10th Annual Cost of Care Report*, Care.com, June 13, 2023, https://www.care.com/c/cost-of-child-care-survey-2023-report/.
13. ReadyNation, "$122 Billion: The Growing Annual Cost of the Infant-Toddler Child Care Crisis," StrongNation, Council for a Strong America, February 3, 2023, https://www.strongnation.org/articles/2038-122-billion-the-growing-annual-cost-of-the-infant-toddler-child-care-crisis.
14. *KIDS COUNT® Data Book: State Trends in Child Well-Being*, Annie E. Casey Foundation, 2023, https://assets.aecf.org/m/resourcedoc/aecf-2023kidscountdatabook-2023.pdf.
15. "Lifting Up Parents' and Providers' Voices and Experiences," RAPID Survey Project, https://rapidsurveyproject.com/.
16. "National Health Expenditures 2022 Highlights," Centers for Medicare and Medicaid Services, Office of the Actuary, fact sheet, December 13, 2023, https://www.cms.gov/newsroom/fact-sheets/national-health-expenditures-2022-highlights.
17. "Total Funding Spent on Public Transit in the U.S.," Statista, https://www.statista.com/statistics/1296052/total-funding-spent-public-transit-us/.
18. Naaz Modan, "Fiscal 2022 K–12 Spending Explained in 6 Charts," K–12 Dive, March 15, 2022, https://www.k12dive.com/news/fiscal-2022-k-12-spending-explained-in-6-charts/620378/.
19. U.S. Department of State, "Progress Report on President

Biden's Climate Finance Pledge," fact sheet, December 2, 2023, https://2021-2025.state.gov/progress-report-on-president-bidens-climate-finance-pledge/#:~:text=Total%20U.S.%20climate%20finance%20increased%20from%20$1.5,and%20$655%20million%20was%20for%20sustainable%20landscapes.

20. Liz Donovan and Muriel Alcorón, "Long Hours, Low Pay, Loneliness and a Booming Industry," *New York Times*, September 25, 2021, www.nytimes.com/2021/09/25/business/home-health-aides-industry.html.
21. M. Zhavoronkova, R. Khattar, and M. Brady, "Occupational Segregation in America," Center for American Progress, March 29, 2022, https://www.americanprogress.org/article/occupational-segregation-in-america/.
22. Claire Cain Miller, "As Women Take Over a Male-Dominated Field, the Pay Drops," *New York Times*, March 18, 2016.
23. Ariane Hegewisch, Miranda Petersen, and Nina Besser Doorley, National Wage Gap Fact Sheet 2024, Institute for Women's Policy Research, September 2024, iwpr.org/wp-content/uploads/2024/09/IWPR-National-Wage-Gap-Fact-Sheet-2024.pdf.
24. Brandon Gomez, "Latinas Lose $1.2 Million Over Their Careers as Wage Gap Persists," CNBC, October 5, 2023, www.cnbc.com/2023/10/05/latinas-lose-1point2-million-over-their-careers-as-wage-gap-persists.html.
25. Ann Garcia and Patrick Oakford, "Unequal Pay Day for Immigrant Women," Center for American Progress, April 9, 2013, https://www.americanprogress.org/article/unequal-pay-day-for-immigrant-women/.
26. "Missing in Action: Immigrant Women's Pay Disparities in the Workforce," Upwardly Global, May 2025, https://www.upwardlyglobal.org/wp-content/uploads/2025/05/upwardlyglobal_EPI_final.pdf.
27. Jonathan Rothwell and Andre M. Perry, "How Racial Bias in Appraisals Affects the Devaluation of Homes in Majority-Black Neighborhoods," Brookings Institution, *Brookings Metro*,

December 5, 2022, https://www.brookings.edu/articles/how-racial-bias-in-appraisals-affects-the-devaluation-of-homes-in-majority-black-neighborhoods/.

28. United Nations High Commissioner for Refugees, "Key Indicators," Refugee Data Finder, last updated June 12, 2025, https://www.unhcr.org/refugee-statistics.

CHAPTER 4: INVISIBLE WALLS

1. "2021 Global Multidimensional Poverty Index (MPI): Unmasking Disparities by Ethnicity, Caste and Gender," United Nations Development Programme, October 7, 2021.
2. Swagata Sarkar, "Depressed and Ostracized: Scrutinizing the Condition of Dalit Women in India and Their Fight for Justice Against Barbarism," *Contemporary Voice of Dalit*, November 9, 2023, https://journals.sagepub.com/doi/abs/10.1177/2455328X231179813.
3. "Indian Women's Literacy Rate Increased by 68% Since Independence: Report," *Mint*, March 15, 2023, https://www.livemint.com/news/india/womens-literacy-rate-increased-by-68-since-independence-report-11678863594186.html.
4. S. Rukmini, "India's Unequal University System," *Mint*, September 10, 2019, https://www.livemint.com/news/india/still-too-few-dalits-in-indian-colleges-1568013598781.html.
5. Sophie Landrin, "India's Elite Schools See a Wave of Suicides Among Dalit Students," *Le Monde* (English edition), September 27, 2023.
6. "Student Suicides: Too Young to Die—Understanding Suicide Causes," *Frontline (The Hindu)*, September 21, 2023, https://frontline.thehindu.com/the-nation/education/student-suicides-too-young-to-die-understanding-suicide-causes/article67314790.ece.
7. Ajay Kumar, "Sexual Violence Against Dalit Women: An Analytical Study of Intersectionality of Gender, Caste, and Class in India," *Journal of International Women's Studies* 22, no. 11

(2021): 4, https://vc.bridgew.edu/cgi/viewcontent.cgi?article=2680&context=jiws.

8. Claudiney Pereira, "Ethno-Racial Poverty and Income Inequality in Brazil," CEQ Working Paper No. 60, CEQ Institute, Tulane University, November 2016.
9. Sasha Yeutseyeva and Thibaud Deguilhem, "Race, Gender and Poverty: Evidence from Brazilian Data," MPRA Paper No. 114411, MPRA, August 2022, https://mpra.ub.uni-muenchen.de/114411/1/MPRA_paper_114411.pdf.
10. Amnesty International, "Myanmar: Four Years After Coup, World Must Demand Accountability for Atrocity Crimes," press release, January 31, 2025, https://www.amnesty.org/en/latest/news/2025/01/myanmar-four-years-after-coup-world-must-demand-accountability-for-atrocity-crimes/.
11. Daniel P. Sullivan, "Paths of Assistance: Opportunities for Aid and Protection Along the Thailand–Myanmar Border," Refugees International, Washington, DC, July 12, 2022.
12. J. Greco, "Refugees in U.S. Struggle to Find Long-Term Work," *Cornell Chronicle*, February 7, 2022, https://news.cornell.edu/stories/2022/02/refugees-us-struggle-find-long-term-work.

CHAPTER 5: CHANGE THE RULES OF THE GAME

1. Tamar Jacoby, "Living in Limbo: Displaced Ukrainians in Poland," Migration Policy Institute, November 2, 2022, https://www.migrationpolicy.org/article/living-limbo-displaced-ukrainians-poland.
2. "Amendment on the Law on Assistance to Ukrainian Citizens in Connection with the Armed Conflict on the Territory of the Country Has Entered into Force." Government of Poland, 2022, https://www.gov.pl/web/udsc-en/the-law-on-assistance-to-ukrainian-citizens-in-connection-with-the-armed-conflict-on-the-territory-of-the-country-has-entered-into-force.
3. Jacoby, "Living in Limbo."
4. Organisation for Economic Co-operation and Development, "What We Know About the Skills and Early Labour Market Outcomes of Refugees from Ukraine," OECD Policy Responses

on the Impacts of the War in Ukraine, January 6, 2023, https://www.oecd.org/content/dam/oecd/en/publications/reports/2023/01/what-we-know-about-the-skills-and-early-labour-market-outcomes-of-refugees-from-ukraine_e95955bf/c7e694aa-en.pdf.

5. UNHCR Polska, "PRESENTATION 2nd Edition: 'Analysis of the Impact of Refugees from Ukraine on the Economy of Poland,'" YouTube livestream, June 10, 2025, at 1:44:07, https://www.youtube.com/live/NaT2jAIgOkw.
6. Sekou Keita and Helen Dempster, "Five Years Later, One Million Refugees Are Thriving in Germany," *Center for Global Development* (blog), December 4, 2020, https://www.cgdev.org/blog/five-years-later-one-million-refugees-are-thriving-germany.
7. Institute for Employment Research (IAB), "Syrian Workers in Germany," European Commission Directorate-General for Migration and Home Affairs, January 8, 2025, https://home-affairs.ec.europa.eu/whats-new/publications/institute-employment-research-iab-syrian-workers-germany_en?prefLang=it.
8. Michael Jarman, "GDP and Refugees: An Economic Argument for Accepting Refugees," *Marriott Student Review* 2, no. 2 (2018): Article 10, https://scholarsarchive.byu.edu/marriottstudentreview/vol2/iss2/10.
9. Jennifer Gordon, "Decent Work for Displaced People: Lessons from the Experiences of Venezuelan Migrant and Refugee Workers in Colombia and Brazil," International Labour Organization Research Brief, January 15, 2024, https://ssrn.com/abstract=4709229.

CHAPTER 7: RESHAPE NORMS

1. "Girls' Education," UNICEF, n.d., https://www.unicef.org/education/girls-education.
2. Khouloud Haskouri, "Access to Education for Rural Moroccan Girls Jumps 34 Points in 20 Years," *Morocco World News*, October 18, 2021, moroccoworldnews.com/2021/10/53906

/access-to-education-for-rural-moroccan-girls-jumps-34-points-in-20years/.

3. Near East Foundation, "Near East Foundation Project PACREP Part 1," YouTube video, March 5, 2020, at 12:34, https://www.youtube.com/watch?v=_0QbOLHiGF4.

CHAPTER 8: SOLIDARITY

1. "The Gender Gap in Land Rights," Food and Agriculture Organization of the United Nations, 2018, https://openknowledge.fao.org/server/api/core/bitstreams/4966d50c-233b-43a9-8fa7-8d43263dd082/content.
2. Shihana Mohamed, "Breaking Down Barriers to Women's Land Rights Starts in Our Homes," *Global Issues*, March 22, 2024, https://www.globalissues.org/news/2024/03/22/36300.
3. ATTAC Maroc, "The Soulaliyate Movement: Moroccan Women Fighting Land Dispossession," War on Want, August 14, 2020, https://waronwant.org/news-analysis/soulaliyate-movement-moroccan-women-fighting-land-dispossession.

Index

About the Author

Jina Krause-Vilmar is a global leader in advancing the economic power of refugee and immigrant women, with two decades of experience shaping research, policy, and systems change across Africa, the Middle East, Latin America, Asia, Europe, and the United States. A pioneer in examining the intersections of women's economic power, displacement, and the prevention of gender-based violence, she has drafted policy language and global standards for the United Nations' interagency coordination bodies, the U.S. Department of State, and the United Nations Refugee Agency (UNHCR). Her published operational guidance has helped governments and humanitarian organizations design gender-inclusive economic development programs that strengthen livelihoods while safeguarding women's rights.

Jina has partnered with national and local governments worldwide to implement frameworks for refugee inclusion, ensuring that women's economic participation is recognized as both a protection tool and a catalyst for community well-being. As the former CEO of Upwardly Global, she led a team of more than one hundred staff and expanded immigrant and refugee workforce inclusion initiatives nationwide—while also helping shape the future of work through inclusive AI strategies. She advised on—and helped secure—bipartisan support for legislation that culminated in the New Deal for New Americans Act in the United States.

She currently serves as the executive director of the Families and Workers Fund and on the steering committee of the Kizuna Network, a feminist organization dedicated to amplifying the leadership, safety, and rights of refugee women leaders. Her work has earned her awards from *Worth*'s Worthy 100, the Female Factor, and other global platforms. Jina's commentary and analysis have appeared in *The New York Times*, *The Guardian*, *Time*, and CNN, and she has been featured on MSNBC, CNBC, and other major news outlets.

Born in New York City and raised in Texas by her Indian mother, Jina learned early on that circumstance, race, and gender do not determine a person's value or potential. Those lived experiences shaped her lifelong commitment to reimagining systems of power and expanding economic opportunity for women pushed to society's margins. She holds a bachelor's degree in government from the University of Texas at Austin, a master of science degree in comparative politics from the London School of Economics, and a certificate in political studies from the University of Aix-Marseille.

Jina now lives in Brooklyn with her family, continuing her work to ensure that when the most vulnerable rise, we all rise.

MOMENT
OF LIFT
BOOKS

Moment of Lift Books, created by Melinda French Gates in partnership with Flatiron Books, is an imprint dedicated to publishing original nonfiction by visionaries working to unlock a more equal world for women and girls.

To learn more about Moment of Lift Books, visit momentoflift.com.